Ending Up Creative

Ending Up Creative

MY SEARCH FOR RENEWAL
THROUGH THE ARTS

A MEMOIR

J. WILLIAM THOMPSON

Drawings by the Author

Ending Up Creative

BOOKS THAT REMEMBER
Washington, D. C.

9 8 7 6 5 4 3 2 1
First Edition

Printed in the United States of America.
ISBN 979-8-9876540-0-2 (paperback)
ISBN 979-8-9876540-2-6 (e-book)

Book cover and interior design by Jonathan Sainsbury.

FOR ANN
Still beside me on this journey

I see the way of the artist as a kind of pilgrimage. When you go on a pilgrimage, you set out from where you happen to be and start walking toward a place of great sanctity in the hope of returning from it renewed, enriched, and sanctified.

However far you may walk, every pilgrimage is a safari into your own dark interior, an inner journey.

—FREDERICK FRANCK, *Art as a Way*

CHAPTER

CHAPTER I

Into the White Wind

I have always known
That at last I would
Take this road, but yesterday
I did not know that it would be today.
—Ariwara no Narihira

"I had the strangest dream," I tell my wife, Ann, in the cold light of a New Hampshire morning. "I dreamed I was under attack."

I often have vivid dreams, but this one seems so out of place, here in the tranquil, majestic White Mountains. The imagery of the dream is already fading, but I recall something about fighter jets in attack formation, armed to the teeth like the F-15s that patrolled the skies over our home in downtown Washington, DC after the 9/11 attacks. Those nights, awakened in our bed by the scream of the F-15 engines, at least I could reassure myself that they were our fighter jets, protecting us. In last night's dream, though, the fighters were attacking *me*.

It's not the kind of dream you expect to have on vacation, even if this vacation wasn't exactly a choice. To cut staff expenses during the great recession, everyone in our association of landscape architects has to take a week's furlough. So Ann and I chose the mountains of New Hampshire, a place we've never seen, and I just had that dream.

There's been plenty of turbulence back at the office in Washington, DC, but I'm not going to dwell on that today. I'm eager to take in the view from the summit of Mount Washington, which I'm told is breathtaking. You can see four states from up there, they say.

Most of the tension back at the association—no surprise—is about money. We are in the middle of the recession of 2008, and the association is so strapped for cash that every staff member had to take a week's "vacation" without pay. One reason for the shortfall is that paid registration is down for the upcoming annual meeting of the association in Denver. Landscape architects can't justify the expense in a downturn, but the association is stuck with the bill for the annual meeting nonetheless.

Another ominous sign is that the chief financial officer, Gerry, has abruptly resigned, giving only two weeks' notice. Gerry has long had financial disagreements with the executive of the association, whom I'll call Patricia. Still, leaving on such short notice is unheard of in a senior staff position. Gerry once told me he planned to give six months' notice to allow a search committee to recruit a replacement. So yes, there's enough turbulence going on in the office to justify that threatening dream.

It may seem a little ironic, then, that I'd settle on Mount Washington for my furlough. The weather on the summit is dangerously erratic, partly because of the vertical rise of the mountain, combined with its north-south orientation; these two features make the range a significant barrier to westerly winds. Hurricane-force gusts are observed from the summit on average of 110 days per year, and the mountain holds records for surface wind speed—231 miles per hour.

Still, I have never visited New Hampshire, and the White Mountains are an area of rare natural beauty. Artists of the Victorian era, including the great painter of American landscapes, Albert Bierstadt, often painted here.

On this blue-sky October morning, Ann and I pile into one of the "stages," actually a late model van. As our driver steers our stage along the steep, winding road up the mountain, the spectacular scenery wipes all thoughts of the office and its turmoil out of my mind. I'm a nature lover to my bones, a lover of both the grand vistas and the intimate morphology of a flower. My love of nature extends to the gardens and parks that humans have created for their own delight and refreshment. This is why my job, as the editor of the association's landscape magazine, headquartered back in Washington, is the best job in the world for me. I've been at the magazine twenty years now and have loved every day of it—well, except the office politics—and for the last ten years I've served as editor in chief, overseeing a monthly magazine that has proved to be a resource and an inspiration for professional landscape architects and anyone interested in gardens, plazas, and other designed landscapes.

Now I'm of retirement age but I'm dithering about the proper time to announce my departure. I have never wanted to hang on until the bitter end, every year showing a little less energy and a little less passion for the work every year for the magazine I love. An additional factor is Gerry's resignation. He was my trusted adviser on the intricacies of the annual budget, and I always said that when he left, I'd do well to follow. Still, I'm scared of stepping out into the void of retirement. How can I possibly replace the creative fulfilment I found in editing the landscape magazine?

As we drive ever higher and it gets ever colder up the mountain, the vegetation grows progressively more sparse and more stunted, as if we were traveling northward on an arc across the continent of North America. Finally our driver calls out, "Welcome to the Arctic!" as we summit into a realm of white—not just snow on the ground, but dense white fog in every direction and a fierce wind blowing. We exit the van, and the wind slams into us, making it hard to walk, hard to stand up in the brunt of it. Everyone, Ann included, seeks shelter in the visitor's center, but I stay outside, fighting the disappointment welling up in me, trying to salvage something from this white violence that's such a far cry from what I had so righteously expected.

Absolutely nothing is visible of the world below—no long views, no spectacular vistas of distant states. I can see a few yards in front of my face, nothing more. Even walking around in this whiteness would be a danger to life and limb, because where does the mountain drop off? I can't see that either.

Back at the lodge this evening, I check my messages. There's one from Lisa, my managing editor, that contains news from the office that wouldn't wait. Reading it goes off like a bombshell behind my eyes.

My dream, apparently, was picking up on some impending threat at the office after all. A small act of interoffice chicanery has torn at the fabric of my beloved magazine on the most iconic page of any magazine: the cover. The annual meeting of the association is coming up, and the association's publisher, whom I'll call Phyllis, marched into the editorial offices and—without me there to stop her—demanded that an announcement for the annual meeting be put on the cover without my knowledge. No one on my staff had the clout to stand up to her.

A small announcement on the cover may seem a minor issue, but our landscape magazine has always followed the lead of fine-art magazines in devoting the entire cover to one compelling image—no text at all except for the magazine's logo. A block of text announcing the meeting of the association will stand out like a foreign object. More broadly, when an editor doesn't have autonomy over the editorial content of a magazine, including the cover, he or she is no longer an editor. Something has to be done to avert this hostile takeover—or I'll be following Gerry out the door sooner than expected.

An experienced, hard-charging marketing director, Phyllis came on board a few years earlier and quickly won the confidence of Patricia. Early on, Phyllis seemed to view me as a valued ally and asset. She had helped raise my profile with such initiatives as a "meet the editor" session at our annual meetings. At the same time, however, she began consolidating a power base of departments and products within the association. A seismic shift came about a year ago, when Phyllis persuaded Patricia to appoint her publisher of the magazine, ostensibly to grow the advertising revenue of the magazine, on which the association depended.

The day Patricia announced Phyllis's new status before the officers of the association, Phyllis sat there looking like the cat that just ate the canary, while I sat there feeling very much like the canary. My immediate worry was that Phyllis would attempt to increase ad revenue by commercializing the editorial content. Historically, advertising and editorial were separate domains, and I had spent years reinforcing the image of the magazine as "the honest broker of information." If advertising began to impinge on the magazine's editorial content— if, for example, the magazine began touting a playground or paving manufacturer in an article, that trust would quickly evaporate. So I climbed the stairs to my office and called the chair of my editorial board, the dean of a prestigious school of architecture, whom I trusted. I thought I should quit then and there, I told him. He advised me to stay the course, that the firewall might yet hold. It was advice he would later recant.

I didn't have to wait long for Phyllis to make her presence felt. She began urging me to embed favorable mentions of products in our articles, which I saw as a slippery slope toward articles that would be thinly veiled advertisements. I gently fended off her requests, reassured that Patricia would remain neutral on matters of editorial policy, as she had up to now. But Phyllis's demands were becoming more and more insistent—and I, it should be known, have no talent for office infighting, just a stubborn inclination to stick by a few core principles. Not long before I left for the White Mountains, Phyllis asked me to stop by her office. She seemed very excited—a clear sign that something dire was afoot.

"I've had the most fabulous idea," she said. "I'm going to invite the CEOs of the most prestigious residential landscape design firms in the country—the best of the best—to put together portfolios of their highest profile luxury home and estate landscapes. I'll convince them to spend serious money on top-level professional photographers. They'll bring the portfolios to you in Denver, and you can pick and choose which projects to publish— no pressure. I know you're always looking for new material, so I thought, 'Bill will love this.'"

There were no windows open in Phyllis's office, but I suddenly felt a terrible chill. Her "fabulous idea" contained multiple pitfalls, but the one that concerned me most was that she had begun aggressively moving to shape editorial content and wasn't even trying to hide it. When I politely declined her "fabulous idea," a dark shadow seemed to fall over Phyllis's face.

"I'm sorry you're not interested in some great new material," she said, her voice icy. "Well, then, we'll just plan our usual 'Meet the Editor' event at the annual meeting. We don't want to get too innovative, do we?"

The chill stayed with me long after I left Phyllis's office. Our standoff had entered a new and dangerous phase. Still, I never would have dreamed that a colleague would make a move against me while I was on furlough. But Phyllis's move was exquisitely timed—she acted just as the magazine was going to press.

The morning after getting the bad news, I phone Patricia. Will her hands-off policy toward editorial content still hold? But this time, she doesn't pick up the phone. I leave a voice message reminding her that changes to the cover of any magazine should never happen without the editor's consent. She emails me back that this was "an emergency"—annual meeting registrations being down, a notice on the cover was needed to encourage members to come to Denver.

This email confirms that an earthquake is in process. Patricia has abandoned her neutrality and the ground has just opened under my feet.

Back at the office in Washington DC, everything feels so different. This building, which used to be my spiritual home, the seat of my creative midlife flowering, has morphed into something alien.

Patricia is eating her lunch, and I'm standing in the door of her office, fuming.

"I need to talk to you." I blurt out. Patricia gives me a searching look. She knows exactly why I'm here and why I'm angry.

"Let me finish my lunch," she says. "I'll come up to your office."

I'm facing a Rubicon moment. Last night, I decided to break ranks, to see if I could bring important board members and fellows of the association over to my cause. That, of course, would amount to direct insubordination and launch an internal war that could backfire horribly. But my gut told me that things were already plenty ugly, so I placed a phone call to enlist the support of the elected president of the association, whom I'll call Jim, at home in the Midwest. I tell him I was on the point of quitting and why. Could he and the board of trustees offer me formal assurances that nothing like this would ever happen again, that my editorial autonomy would be inviolate from here on out?

Jim waffled. "Give me a couple of weeks," he said. "I need to talk to all the board of trustees to sound out their feelings. Of course, they may just say that Bill's on his high horse." And I knew right then that Jim and the board were not going to have my back. The association was all about maintaining the status quo and a stable hierarchy and, with my criticism of the executive, I was threatening to overturn that.

That was my last card to play. It failed, and now I know that I can't win this battle. But I still have choices. Nobody's firing me. I could stay in place in my corner office, draw my comfortable salary, and wait for the next shoe to fall—the next small slicing away of respect that I know will come. Right now, though, all I feel is betrayed, and all I see is one way out.

"I'm giving notice," I say, when Patricia comes in and shuts the door. I tell her why I'm quitting in no uncertain terms. "I will see the October issue through till it goes to press. And I will not meet with Phyllis for any reason."

"That text on the cover was a one-time event," Patricia declares. *(Yeah, right, until the next "crisis.")* "But," she adds, "I never discourage anyone from giving notice." With that, she gets up and exits the office—and it's over.

Just like that, the most important and most fulfilling phase of my working life has come to a close. Granted, I am of retirement age, but I would have liked to have planned to retire gracefully, with a farewell party and the usual expressions of gratitude for my years of service. *(No champagne toasts for you, old boy!)* Instead, I'll just close the door behind me when I leave, and that will be it.

My last few weeks at the office are surreal. It's as if I'm in quarantine—hardly any of my colleagues from other departments stop by my office to say they were glad to have worked with me. I stop attending Monday morning staff meetings. My small magazine staff, bless their hearts, does give me a farewell party at a local restaurant.

Then we ship the October issue, and I walk out of the building in downtown Washington, never to return. This is goodbye.

CHAPTER 2

The Great Passage

Old men ought to be explorers
Here or there does not matter
We must be still and still moving
Into another intensity
For a further union, a deeper communion....
In my end is my beginning.
    —T.S. Eliot, *Four Quartets*

Society is littered with retired men who suffer from apathy and depression because their identity was so tied to their work. My identity certainly was. So am I likely to start drinking heavily or have trouble getting out of the bed in the morning? Thankfully not. Job or no job, I have a good safety net in my life. Having salted away part of my salary into stable investments, I have no money worries. Although in my late sixties, my health is generally good. Ann and I own a comfortable yellow brick townhouse, fully paid for, in the historic core of Washington.

Yes, I would have preferred a graceful retirement, but

that wasn't in the cards. I did leave the magazine with my self-respect mostly intact. One day, walking through Meridian Hill Park, I run into a former ad rep for the magazine. He begins fulminating about Phyllis, who managed to get him fired. But I steer off his diatribe. "I'd rather focus," I tell him, "on the twenty great years I had at the magazine than on how it all came to an end."

Those years were very precious to me, and all the more precious because that success arrived so late in my working life, just when I had begun to feel that I'd thrown my life away.

In my midforties I had ended up in the little dead-end town of Walhalla, South Carolina, which to me felt like a place where losers came to give up. I had ended up there to be near Mom's extended family and where I could live in one of my uncle's houses rent free.

Walhalla's saving grace is its setting at the foot of the Blue Ridge Mountains, where thickets of mountain laurel and rhododendron grace the hillsides. There, the wild and scenic Chattooga River, where the movie *Deliverance* was filmed, still runs free. All my forebears had homesteaded in those mountains generations back. I had roots.

What I didn't have was a career I could love—and it wasn't as if I hadn't been trying really hard to find one. What I had always wanted to do, since I was a child, was to write; to craft true stories of people, places, and events in the manner of writers of the American landscape such as Bill Bryson, Wendell Berry, and John McPhee. The most likely route to that dream would have been to find a job with a magazine or newspaper, but my initial attempts to find a career in mainstream journalism yielded nothing, and I lacked a strategy or the grit to continue a long job search. I did place the occasional freelance piece in mainstream periodicals, but again, I didn't have a coherent strategy to turn freelancing into a career. Instead I drifted into teaching remedial reading to adults, a line of work for which I had little taste and from which I finally crashed and burned in my late thirties. The abrupt end turned out to be a blessing, forcing me to consider what I really wanted to do with the rest of my life. I began madly thrashing around to forge a career that I could love, no matter what it took.

Somewhere I read a statistic that landscape architecture was one of the up-and-coming career choices. Almost by happenstance I came upon a three-year master's degree in landscape architecture at the University of Georgia for adults who lacked a design background. I didn't know much about gardens and nothing about design, but I had always loved the outdoors and thought a career in preserving the environment would be right up my alley. I visited the program in Athens, Georgia, and was immediately seduced by the big, colorful design drawings the students had pinned on the walls of the design studio. The faculty adviser I spoke to made the transition to a radically new career sound so easy. (How painfully misleading that would turn out to be.)

Truth is, studying landscape architecture was arguably the silliest thing I could have done. My lack of experience in any field of design or gardening would prove a massive disadvantage. And it only look a few lackluster semesters to confirm that I had no native talent for the technical aspects of grading and drainage, the layout of low-speed roads, irrigation calculations, or the precise technical drawings. Even the artistic side of design was a challenge. As a child I had shown a precocious talent for drawing, but that talent had atrophied for lack of use.

At that precarious juncture, my love of the written word emerged as my only saving grace. Could it be there was a role for me as the John McPhee of landscape architecture? I spent hours in the school's reading room (when I should have been working at the drafting table) poring through the literature of landscape architecture, all the way back to Frederick Law Olmsted. I devoured the articles in the magazine published by the association of landscape architects. Finally, I helped to found a quarterly student magazine, for which I became editor and garnered a National Endowment for the Arts (NEA) grant. I loved working with a student team to assign articles on regional landscape projects, lay out the pages, and work with the printer. If I couldn't be a John McPhee of landscape architecture, maybe there could be another role for me in the publishing side of the profession.

When I walked out of the university, degree in hand, however, I quickly discovered that there wasn't a landscape architecture office in the country that needed an aspiring writer of the American landscape on staff. What they needed were skilled draftspersons with knowledge of design and the technical aspects of grading, drainage, and all the rest of those areas in which I was only minimally competent. I crisscrossed the Southeast being politely turned away by one design office after another. Finally, I gambled my last tank of gas on driving to Houston, Texas, where I'd read that a consortium was planning a heavy-rail transit line. I'd done my final thesis on designing pedestrian access to rail stations, so they hired me.

My hard-won career opening was short lived: the city held a referendum, and the rail project was voted out of existence. There was nothing left but to scuttle back to the South Carolina, where my extended family took me in. I was lucky enough to land a job teaching technical writing in a nearby university, but it only paid a living wage and had to be renewed (or not) year by year. By now, I was forty-six years old and teetering on a prospect of a series of transient teaching jobs across the South for the rest of my working years. I hadn't spent three years studying landscape architecture for this.

So on this desperate afternoon, I picked up the phone and made that cold call to the landscape architecture magazine I'd read so often in the reading room at the landscape department at the University of Georgia. I had absolutely no expectation that the small editorial staff in Washington, DC would have an opening for me, but this was my last card to play. So imagine how amazed I was when the editor herself, Susan, picked up and said the magic words: "Are you looking for a position?"

It turned out that the editorial staff was in a phase of upheaval. Susan was being forced out, so it was an act of extraordinary kindness for her to bother with my needs at all. Susan gave me some pointers on how make contact with the incoming editor, a millionaire art collector brought on board to transform the magazine into a glossy, high profile display of the profession's best work. The long-term goal was to appeal to a mass-market audience. When I spoke to the editor, Jim, he flew me up to Washington and hired me over lunch.

At age forty-six, I had finally found the work it seemed I had been born to do. The feeling can only be described as pent-up deliverance, especially if you have had too many years of missteps and dead ends in search of a job you could love and throw your whole strength behind. As if someone had just popped a cork in my brain, words, sentences, and whole paragraphs came flooding out. Writing about designed landscapes became a complete creative flowering for me. I was head over heels in love with this magazine in transition and its small readership almost entirely of working landscape architects.

Work time, suddenly, was sacred time. I came into the office nights and weekends and during snowstorms to work on articles. I volunteered for every writing assignment, no matter how far flung or seemingly insignificant. "Late bloomer" doesn't even begin to describe my state. It was rebirth. I had just started out on my life's work—which was all the more precious given how improbable it was that I would ever find it. But I did find it. I am living, breathing proof that a middle-aged career changer can find the calling of his dreams.

That's all behind me now, much as I cherish the memory of my twenty years at the magazine. Still, there is no denying that I'm carrying around a residue of disappointment about the way my career ended. But there must be some way, even for a 67-year old, to get that out of his system—or mostly out of his system. So how does a 334-mile bicycle ride sound?

It's not as outlandish as it sounds. I've been an avid cyclist most of my adult life. I still ride every day, and I can still pull a good day's miles. What makes the proposed ride more attractive is that the bike trail is almost all completely off road, from Pittsburgh back home to DC. The first leg of the ride will be on a converted railroad bed, now named the Great Allegheny Passage, and then on to the (Chesapeake & Ohio) C&O Canal Towpath. Surely five days of riding unencumbered by traffic and city noise should be the ticket for calming and meditative healing. Even that iconic name of the trail –the Great Passage—hints at transformation.

I buy a long-wheelbase Burley recumbent for its comfortable seating position that will reduce fatigue on long days of pedaling. Ann insists that I find a companion on the trail in case of an accident, and I locate Dale, another retiree recumbent enthusiast, on a cycling website. We load the recumbents in Dale's van, and his wife drops us off in Pittsburgh in early June.

There is something enormously freeing and exhilarating about setting off on a long bicycle trip. The ribbon of crushed stone on the converted rail bed beckons you on, you breathe deep of the open air, free of automobile exhaust, and there is nothing else that will cover the miles ahead of you other than the smooth motion of your own legs spinning the pedals.

Dale never talks while riding, but over dinner in a café along the trail I learn a bit about his career in the Maryland statehouse and, more darkly, his obsessive hatred of his sister. "My greatest wish is to piss on my sister's grave," Dale shares, apparently unaware of how bizarre that sounds to someone he's known only a few days. The hatred is rooted, apparently, in the sibling resentment around their parents' buying her a house and car after she had flamed out of college after a steady diet of parties and recreational drugs. (Dale of course had to work his own way through college and always pay for everything by the sweat of his brow.)

Listening to Dale spill out his sibling rage, I sense what a dark burden it must be for him to carry that rage through his life. I hope to never nourish that kind of resentment toward anyone, but specifically toward Patricia or Phyllis.

The long hours of silent pedaling behind Dale's long-wheelbase recumbent have the potential for profound boredom. I rarely see another rider and only occasionally pass through a village. The trail is almost always shrouded in a green womb of deep woods along a series of slow-moving rivers. The changes of scene seem minute. Then I start seeing the nuances. In Pennsylvania, the path is a converted railroad bed surfaced with wonderfully smooth crushed stone. In Maryland, the canal towpath is a rutted, muddy track built for mules that towed the now-extinct canal boats. As long as we are in Pennsylvania, a fast-flowing river, the Youghiogheny, is on our left. When we descend into Maryland, the mighty Potomac is on our right. So, instead of succumbing to daydreams and letting my mind obsess about the past, I find that my attention becomes clearer and sharper as I notice the changes in rock outcrops and in the forest canopy. And with that focus on my surroundings, my thoughts begin to find their place in quietness and my resentment toward Patricia, in particular, begins to lose its serrated edge and I see her and myself as players in a larger pattern.

Looking back, I should not have been totally surprised at the way my editorship came to an end. For the ten years I'd served as top editor, I'd followed my vision to create a vibrant magazine that would truly serve working landscape architects. What I didn't understand was that my single focus on editorial content was not enough to make me indispensable. For one thing, I had no aptitude for the business side of putting out a magazine and, strange as this may seem, I never made any attempt to educate myself in such crucial areas as the editorial budget. I was given a generous allowance for hiring good freelance writers and photographers, and I was careful to finish each fiscal year with a healthy surplus. I spent money on a tactical, issue-by-issue basics, never thinking there was a need for an overall plan.

This all came to a head in an all-staff financial planning session where Patricia asked me to share the details of the editorial budget for the coming fiscal year. What, for example, was I planning to do with the budgetary surplus—fold it back into the overall association budget? I don't remember what I said in the meeting, but I was excruciatingly aware that I was floundering in front of the entire staff. Patricia said not a word but simply watched me with a faint, detached smile on her face.

Another blind spot was my failure to understand that the editor of an association magazine should be a public face of the association, which meant dressing for success and schmoozing with leaders of related organizations. To me, this was all irrelevant to fulfilling my mission of ensuring great editorial content, whereas to Patricia, such public appearances were central to the editor's role. Our difference of opinion became glaringly obvious at a meeting of a government bureau on Capitol Hill, one of those meetings that are long on formality and short on meaningful content. I arrived in the neat business casual attire I wore at the office and took a seat next to Patricia.

"You're not dressed for the occasion, Bill," she noted, and indeed, everyone else at the meeting was dressed to the nines. But her comment irked me. Wasn't Patricia aware of the work I was doing to connect the editorial content with the needs of the readers? Didn't she know how hard I had worked with writers, photographers, and my own editorial staff to publish in-depth editorial content month after month? Didn't she share my vision of giving the magazine back to the profession?

Well no, she probably didn't, and I now realize that I never took the trouble to make her aware of it. I could have made a trusted ally of my boss, as every good employee should. I could have requested periodic meetings to explain my evolving vision for the magazine, thank her for solving any problems, and gently tease out areas where I might help in refining the brand of the association. Instead, I held Patricia at arm's length, fearful that any conversations with her would encourage her to request changes in editorial direction that I couldn't accept.

Still, would anything I said or did differently have changed the eventual outcome? In the words of Lyle Lovett's sad love song:

> *If the stars didn't shine on the water*
> *Then the sun wouldn't burn on the sand*
> *And if I were the man that she wanted*
> *I would not be the man that I am.*

I was a man with an absolute passion for words and an unshakable faith that publishing good information could move this beloved profession forward. I wasn't an all-purpose manager who could play multiple roles—social, financial, sartorial. Patricia, by contrast, was a tenacious association executive who, as far as I could tell, never had any great interest in landscape architecture beyond the governance of the association, growing its numbers and influence, and raising its "brand" as an association. The amazing thing is that we coexisted peaceably for nearly a decade. And yes, I am enormously grateful for those years.

At Harper's Ferry, Dale's wife picks him up and I continue on, happy to be alone. Climbing up from the towpath into the heart of a DC neighborhood, I feel like Dr. Livingston, emerging from the depths of long sojourn in an African forest. And what a joy to see Ann's broad smile as she opens the front door to greet me!

I met Ann twenty years ago at the Friends Meeting of Washington, the day I had decided would likely be my last Quaker meeting. Although I knew nothing of Quakers growing up, I had recently been attending Sunday morning Meetings for Worship, attracted by a religion that valued meditative silence over dogma and sermonizing. But as a relative newcomer to Washington, about to turn fifty but eager to find a community, I was having trouble connecting with the inward-looking Quakers, whom I misinterpreted as standoffish introverts.

This Meeting for Worship, however, had an energy unlike any I'd experienced. Quaker Meetings, at their best, are characterized by the deep meditative silence in which each attendee centers down into him or herself. But this Sunday, a book entitled *The Bell Curve* had just come out, and an African American gentleman stood up in the meeting room and began inveighing against the research which attempted to portray African Americans as innately inferior to whites. Others in the meeting echoed his outrage, and the meeting exploded into spoken messages charged with vitriol.

At the Rise of Meeting I sat almost stunned in my pew when I noticed a dark-eyed woman sitting next to me. We briefly shared responses to the brouhaha, after which I offered, "Would you like to continue this over coffee?" and we repaired to a coffee shop on Connecticut Avenue. I didn't know it then, but my fate was sealed that day.

To be clear, I was a lonely divorcée looking for companionship in a faceless city, but I wasn't looking to remarry, ever. My first wife, Helen, was a lovely Englishwoman with whom I had two children, but our union was probably doomed from the start, for reasons that I will explain later. I'd come out of the divorce leery of any further commitments—once bitten, twice shy, as they say.

But after a year of dating Ann, I couldn't deny that something was happening to me. Then we took a trip to Portugal, and Ann was introduced to my quirky travel habits—rambling, seemingly aimless itineraries, bumping down rutted roads in second-class buses, not knowing in what strange lodging we'd sleep the next night. Most women, I am sure, would have high tailed it for home after a couple of days of this, but Ann took it in stride and even seemed to enjoy getting way off the beaten track. If, as they say, traveling together tells you whether two people are compatible, this trip strongly suggested that we were.

So, two years after we met, we were married in a bare-bones Quaker ceremony in a high-ceilinged room in an annex to the main meeting house of that same Friends Meeting. Still gun shy about tying the knot a second time, I couldn't bear to have anything that smacked of a conventional wedding ceremony, not even flower arrangements. It was a bitter cold January day, and we weren't sure who would show up, but my daughter Emily came up from Charlotte and one of Ann's brothers drove down from Massachusetts.

Ann and I had written and memorized our own vows, and we stood facing each other before the small group of friends and family and spoke the vows aloud. Ann went first, looked me in the eye, and spoke hers without a hitch.

Then it was my turn. I was doing fine until I came to the fateful phrase "commit my life to you." There was a terrible pause as I almost choked on the words. Was I actually doing this marriage thing a second time? But something in my heart yanked me back to the present and the life journey Ann and I seemed destined to travel together. I took a deep breath and glory be! I committed. I've never looked back.

These twelve years later, my life with Ann is key to my recovery from the disorientation of retirement. We begin taking marathon walks, at least an hour and a half in length every day. Ann, a long-limbed woman with salt-and-pepper hair, and I, a once-slender, blondish man, now mostly bald, tramp across this beautiful, park-rich city with its miles of historic neighborhoods that invite us to walk forever. Among our favorite treks is a route that takes us through the lovely Tregaron Gardens and then up through a neighborhood of stately old homes to the National Cathedral. These days, we almost always walk arm in arm. We end up overlooking the floral display in the walled Bishop's Garden designed by Frederick Law Olmsted Jr. I feel so lucky to be able to walk through two spectacular gardens in the midst of this dense metropolitan area—and am reminded how my interest in designed landscapes led me to the career I loved all those years.

After our daily walks, Ann and I often end up at our community garden, a collection of a hundred or so organic vegetable plots in the nearby Cleveland Park neighborhood. It's tended by city dwellers, most of whom live in apartments or condominiums and, without their small garden plots, would have no land of their own to tend and cherish. My personal passion is building the soil by burying the vegetable scraps, fish bones, and coffee grounds from our kitchen in the soil, where the natural biota will turn it all into humus. It's my way of reducing our waste stream and putting something back into the Earth. And there's a payoff: the soil has become dark and friable—and fertile—when I turn the shovel in it.

Aside from soil building, though, I've never been much of a gardener. When I first took possession of this plot, my gardening methods were, well, laughable. I tossed out seeds and planted seedlings willy-nilly. Then Ann came into my life and took over, and her upbringing on an Illinois farm kicked in. The plants were all in straight rows, and weeds appeared at the risk of their lives. Suddenly we were reaping home-grown food in abundance—several varieties of peppers and tomatoes, collards and arugula, and, in the cooler months, broccoli and leaf lettuce.

In my present state, still grieving that difficult retirement, the physical labor of the garden has been a life saver. Spreading wheelbarrow loads of mulch releases pent-up energy and focuses the mind totally on the meaningful task at hand. As I straighten up to look around at the dozens of equally verdant gardens, I see an earthly paradise under the blue dome of the sky. This little labor-intensive plot of ground is central to my recovery from the end of a career.

Another key component of my recovery occurs every Sunday at 9 a.m. at my Quaker meeting. Being married under the care of the meeting opened my heart to a warmth of the Quaker community that I hadn't seen before, and the meeting seems more and more to be my rightful spiritual home. In good weather Ann and I can walk to the meeting house from home in less than a half hour, which is a wonderful way to prepare ourselves for the experience of the meeting, so different from almost anything else in our lives in Washington.

The nine o'clock meeting takes place in the same room where Ann and I were married. With its big stone fireplace and timbered rafters, the room resembles a hall in some wilderness lodge. Friends take their seats facing one another in a rough circle in a deep silence that, on most Sunday mornings, will last an entire hour. Very rarely, someone speaks out of the silence, usually to ask the attendees to hold a sick friend or family member "in the Light" or to share some spiritual opening. There is a tacit agreement to not mention politics, which, in this political town, constantly looms as a source of agitation for those of us in search of some degree of inner peace. At the end of the silent worship, called the Rise of Meeting, our small gathering shares the joys and sorrows of their lives since we last met.

Our silent reflection this morning pays homage to the Quaker roots in the 1600s when George Fox preached a radical form of Christianity grounded in direct experience of the sacred. So, from the beginning, this personal religious experience was more important than doctrine or theology. The great difference in our twenty-first century meeting is that so few of us are Christian believers. So in a sense, we are perpetuating the forms of early Quakerism without the central belief that gave it substance. For me, never attracted to theological absolutes, this lack of dogma opens up an enormous space of possibility. It calls me to an inner journey in which I can draw on world religions, the awesome truths of science, the pantheism of Spinoza, and my own inner discoveries along the way.

Having practiced a few forms of meditation over the years, this Sunday morning is a time when I can center down into the truth of that inner journey. Although I'm not looking for a God or any great revelation, I would welcome either if they spontaneously came my way. (They never have.)What I am instead looking for is an hour's respite from my thoughts—regrets and resentments from the recent past, uncertainties about the near future—all those ruminations that seem to clatter around willy-nilly in my head. So I'm relieved, in these Sunday morning meetings, when the deep silence in the room persuades my mind to slow and let its internal chatter find its place of quietness, let my awareness focus on the high-ceilinged room where the sunlight streams in through the French doors and a red cardinal sings its heart out somewhere nearby. In the silence of this small community of Friends there is a lovely spirit, a community of souls coming together, each allowed the space to travel his or her inner journey in a circle of trust.

Having successfully pedaled through the Great Passage, maybe now I can grapple with the looming question: What am I doing with the rest of my life? I'm determined not to degenerate into a comfortable old duffer who alternates between napping in his reclining chair and watching hours of afternoon TV. I have heard, and believed, that retirement should be a time of expansion, not contraction.

I gleaned this notion from, among others, the writings of William Sadler, a Harvard sociologist. Sadler undertook a twelve-year study of two hundred people to determine whether it was possible for older adults to enjoy successful, happy lives in later life. His finding was an emphatic *yes*. He affirmed, with examples, that older adults can continue to make positive life changes and continue to be creative and fulfilled even into their eighties. He cited research that showed that the brain can actually add neurons and dendrites in later life, allowing the right and left hemispheres to productively talk to one another.

So yes, it's theoretically possible for a retired person to live an intense, creatively fulfilling life. The question is whether *I* can live that life. I was born with a deep desire to express myself through the creative arts. These, I sense, represent the most restorative, most life-affirming path for a wounded soul seeking a way to heal—not just to recover from this slump but to climb back singing, to affirm that in my old years I can find the expression that is uniquely mine.

My first and deepest love is writing, but what to write exactly, and for whom? I miss the platform that I had with the magazine. My monthly musings on my editor's page had a readership of thousands who were often sparked to respond with heartfelt letters to the editor. I left that platform of readers behind when I walked out the door of the association. How to replace it, or is finding a new platform even possible?

Other than writing, there are two creative arts in which I already have a foothold. One is the folk art of playing homegrown music with others. The second is the difficult art of drawing and painting the human portrait and figure.

I have been sketching for years and feel that I have a lot of untapped potential in me. But is it too late in my life to do something really fine—to go beyond just sketching and produce something people would want to look at? I don't want to just dip my toe into the arts. I want to dive deep. I understand that means tackling a huge learning curve, both of motor skills and knowledge.

Where to begin that long process, though? One obvious step would be to seek instruction—to find gifted teachers who understand the great traditions of art and how to instruct aspiring artists of any age take part of those traditions.

One retiree who took this approach to its logical conclusion is historian Nell Painter. In her 2018 memoir, *Old in Art School,* Painter chronicles how, after she retired from a very successful career as a history professor and author, she made a major late-life commitment: She enrolled in an undergraduate Bachelor of Fine Arts program in painting at her state university. Not content with earning her BFA, she took on a challenging Master of Fine Arts (MFA) program at the Rhode Island School of Design. While I admire Painter's commitment to the arduous multi-year process of learning to draw and paint, I don't view earning academic degrees as a necessary goal, or even a particularly good path, to producing art that anyone would want to look at.

But I can at least do this much: I can sign up at my first-ever art class at the Art League of Washington.

CHAPTER 3

The Torpedo Factory

What I have not drawn I have never really seen, and when I start drawing an ordinary thing I realize how extraordinary it is.
—Frederick Franck, *The Zen of Seeing*

Hope is in the air as I stand at my easel and drag the stick of vine charcoal across the tooth of the paper, trying to capture a facsimile of the full-figured woman, nude, posing in front of our art class.

I can do this.

And indeed, a reasonable likeness of the model begins to emerge under my fingers. I feel a surge of elation.

I've got the knack.

As we've been doing every week, our small class of figure drawing students, most of them women, has convened in this industrial-scale building where torpedoes were manufactured during World War II which now houses the Art League. Our studio enjoys north light and an overview of the Potomac River.

Can leaving the landscape magazine have had a silver lining? For sure, it has given me time for exploring my creative passions. Now all my mornings and afternoons are free, and I'm going to dive into art—specifically life drawing of the human figure—for all I'm worth.

Life drawing is the centuries-old practice of drawing the human figure from direct observation, with no photos or other artificial aids standing between you and the radical experience of being in the same space as the model for a finite amount of time. Its greatest exponents, arguably, were the great masters of the Italian Renaissance, particularly Leonardo da Vinci, and drawing the figure has since been considered an essential component of an artist's training. The human body is among the most difficult of all subjects to draw. Getting the proportions right in relation to each other, dealing with the perspective of the pose (the dreaded foreshortening), the interplay of light and shadow—there's no reliable key to get it all right except long practice to coordinate your eye and hand.

So here I am in my first art class, ever. But again, I'm not starting from scratch in this art journey. I've been sketching people for years, entirely self-taught—or rather, my only teachers were a couple of important books and a lot of trial and error. I've learned the basic skills of drawing by just doing it—sketching people and places on the street, at musical events, and while traveling. Along the way, I've come to believe that I do have an aptitude, or at least a keen interest, in drawing people.

My purpose at the Art League is to find out whether I can take that interest to the next level. I want to reflect the proportions of the human body accurately, but also drench it in feeling and expression. That's what art is all about, isn't it? I want to make something beautiful.

As I look around the studio, I find myself wondering who among my classmates shares my intensity. And indeed, a few seem to be committed artists who have been working at this for years. Others, I suspect, are looking for something to fill a weekday afternoon, to dabble at life drawing with friends and then go out for lattes and talk about it. More power to them if they enjoy that. Problem is, you can't get very far with drawing the figure by dabbling. It's a very exacting pursuit that requires years of concentrated effort to get good. That's what I'm here for. I'm in this for the long haul, whatever it takes.

Avis, a slight, gray-haired woman who is a seasoned drawing instructor circulates among the easels with words of advice or encouragement. She assumes that you already have a handle on the basics of drawing the figure. The aim of this class is to go beyond the basics, to help us loosen up and learn to draw more freely, more expressively.

Today Avis has given us a special challenge: whoever draws the most convincing and artful life drawing of the model will be awarded "the Diebenkorn Prize," a reference to twentieth-century artist Richard Diebenkorn, who was known for his figure drawings, among other things. The "prize" is not a real award but rather a verbal "attaboy" that says one of us will be first among equals.

On the low stage where Avis has draped cloths and arranged other props, the model takes a dramatic pose. I lean toward my easel and begin sketching with intense concentration. As the figure flows out of my vine charcoal onto the paper, I am confirmed in a growing conviction: I do have a gift for this. But there's something else, a darker, competitive urge. My ego kicks in. I want to be the best in the room.

After twenty minutes, that seem to pass in an instant, Avis calls time and we line up our easels to display our handiwork. Avis moves down the line, carefully studying each before she proclaims, "And the winner of the Diebenkorn Prize is—Bill!"

A honeyed glow of satisfaction wells up in me. *Yes, yes, I am the best, and this proves it!*

My elation is short lived. "I think Sara's drawing is the best," grouses one of the women, and a couple of her cronies take up the complaint. Avis takes another look at Sara's drawing and says, "Very well, then. Bill and Sara will share the Diebenkorn Prize."

Outraged pride surges through me. *I don't want to share! The Diebenkorn Prize is rightfully mine.* But I hold my tongue, as to protest the loss of a make-believe award would be truly asinine.

Still, in this moment I am introduced to that craving for accolades and preeminence—and sour resentment when I don't get them. It's a craving that will prove devilishly hard to shake—or to feed.

Art, I am about to learn, is a journey of self-discovery, not all of it comforting.

As a kid —like so many of us—I loved to draw. There was that book about evolution that I dictated to my mother and illustrated with colorful drawings of dinosaurs and other extinct fauna done in wax crayons—all around the age of nine. My love of drawing flourished until about age twelve, when I noticed that something was missing. I now know that I lacked a basic notion of perspective— that my flattened-out kid's drawings didn't look the way the three-dimensional world really looked. If I had had a good art teacher at that age, I might have gotten over that hurdle, seriously pursued artwork, and made something of it. Instead, I just packed it in.

The itch to draw reemerged in my late thirties while I was studying landscape architecture. I hadn't drawn for so long that the drawings I turned in with assignments were klutzy. I envied the fine perspective sketches of my more advanced fellow students. Nor did my professors offer much encouragement that I would ever be able to draw like that. One old German expat declaimed in his thick accent, "You realize, of course, that your drawing is not up to our high standards?"

That began to change when I took an internship with the Atlanta Bureau of Planning, and the in-house artist saw something—a flame of intense interest, perhaps—in my efforts and encouraged me to show him any sketches I made.

At about the same time I came across a recently published book, *Drawing on the Right Side of the Brain* by Betty Edwards, who assured me that anyone could learn to draw, and draw well. Even the most difficult subjects—portraits and the human figure—were within reach. Edwards referenced an older book, *The Natural Way to Draw,* by Kimon Nicolaïdes. I tracked down the book, the distillation of fifteen years of Nicolaïdes' teaching at the Art Students League in New York. He declared that there is only one way to learn to draw, and that is to see as an artist sees, which involves having a fresh, vivid, physical contact with the object you draw through as many of the senses as possible—and especially through the sense of touch. In short, Nicolaïdes said, *you have to touch the model with your eyes.*

What in the world would that mean in practice? I was about to find out.

There was standing room only on the crowded city bus bound for downtown Atlanta the morning of a working day. I happened to be the one standing, which gave me a good vantage point to view the passengers lucky enough to have seats. And then the thought dawned: Why not now?

I fished a drawing pad and a No. 2 pencil out of my tote bag and scanned the passengers for the most likely subject. I quickly settled on one: an ordinary-looking young woman engrossed in a book directly in my line of sight. It might be the worst possible situation to try out the Nicolaïdes prescription for drawing—or it might be the very best place to start. From my upright vantage point and balancing my drawing pad on one arm, I imagined that my pencil point was touching the "model" instead of the paper. Then, as I slowly moved my eye along the contour, or edge, of the model, I followed with my pencil along the paper. *Be guided more by the sense of touch than the sense of sight,* Nicolaïdes had written. And as if by miracle, a rough likeness of the woman appeared in lines of graphite.

If the "model" had any inkling that I was surreptitiously drawing her, she made no sign. For my part, I felt I was seeing a human face as I never had before: the symmetry of the features, the unique contours of a quite ordinary nose, eyes, and mouth. The image that emerged felt profoundly *me, mine,* together with an intense awareness of the present moment. Key to it all was the sheer improbability of what I seemed to be accomplishing, standing here on a moving bus, accomplishing something unheard of on public transit.

After that, I began drawing without restraint—people sitting on benches, sleeping on benches, sipping coffee in cafés, watching a parade. I never said, "I don't have the time." Instead, I found small chunks of time in my day, I'd draw at coffee breaks, lunch breaks, on the bus ride home, anytime. The more I drew, the better I got, and the better I got, the more I wanted to draw—a virtuous circle.

Although he died in 1938, Nicolaïdes (with a healthy assist from Edwards) became my first and most important drawing teacher, because he taught me how to look intensely enough to "touch" the model with my eyes. I wouldn't take an in-person art class until Avis's, these many years later, and nothing will ever mean as much for my drawing as Nicolaïdes' iconic instruction.

It seems strange, but a key feature of my journey into art is that some of my most important guides have been people I never met.

Back at the Torpedo Factory, I sign up for a second course, portraits in watercolor, thinking that the application of pigment will be essential to raising my artwork to the next level. It's an odd detour, given that I have never had any particular interest in color—I'm a line and form person, period. Still, the instructor comes highly recommended.

The first day of the portrait class, I meet the remarkable Jackie Saunders, a small, wiry eighty-year-old, still brimming with energy and enthusiasm for painting portraits. Although she holds degrees in fine art, she didn't learn this difficult skill in her academic courses but taught herself by emulating a book of the watercolors of Charles Reid, a contemporary American artist.

Today in the studio, a clothed model takes a seat at the front of the room, and we students do our level best to capture some semblance of her features. Jackie prowls the room, stopping to offer a word of caution here, a word of encouragement there. She exhorts us with certain basic premises, including a restatement of Nicolaïdes' "natural" way to draw: "Keep your eye on the model and your pencil on the paper."

Like legions of aspiring artists before me, I'm quickly learning that watercolor is a very slippery medium. Mixing believable skin tones is a major hurdle. Most frustrating of all is to draw a satisfying pencil portrait of the posed model, only to ruin it with a muddy, discolored wash. It will take many months of trial and error to even begin to learn to control this mercurial medium—or rather to give the medium freedom to produce its own surprising results.

Gradually, however, over the weeks of the course I seem to be making progress in applying a credible wash. To my discomfiture, though, Jackie seems to reserve her praise for the most pedestrian efforts (to me, anyway) of my fellow classmates. Stopping at a lopsided scrawl at an easel near mine, she loudly exults, "Oh, that's a beautiful painting. Frame it! Frame it!" When she looks at my effort, by contrast, she says in a low voice, "That's better than last week."

I gradually realize that Jackie is trying to give each

student what he or she needs, even if that means doling out what I consider inappropriate praise. And she may feel that I am less needy of praise than most. (How wrong she is about that!)

The bigger question is: Where did all this need come from—this painful craving for preeminence and accolades?

Honestly, I'm not sure, but it may have its root in the recent collapse of my standing in the professional world. When I was the editor of the landscape magazine, I had a place in the sun that was beyond question. There was, for example, that time at the annual meeting of the association when I was awarded a medal for my writing and editing about landscape architecture. Traditionally, the award ceremony is focused on built landscapes—the creation of outstanding gardens, parks, and plazas, and the awards go to the landscape architects who designed them.

The awards for that year were given out at formal ceremony before the seated audience of hundreds of landscape architects. Each award winner was to walk across a stage to receive his or her award to polite applause from the audience. The next winner garnered more polite applause, and so on. My turn was last, and I walked out on the stage before the assembled audience of the profession. As the president handed me the medal, the entire audience rose in a standing ovation.

The sound of all those clapping hands was the confirmation that I'd earned my professional place in the sun. Going forward, I think I wore my prominence lightly—my foremost goal was to serve the profession that I loved—but that place in the sun was immensely gratifying. Where is that applause now? No hands are clapping anymore. That would be fine except that most retired guys still yearn to be recognized for something. But whoever heard of any older adult with little or no formal art training achieving anything worthwhile in the visual arts?

Actually, I have come across one such adult, Elizabeth Layton, whose extraordinary drawings I first saw at a 1992 solo exhibit at the Smithsonian American Art Museum.

Elizabeth was a very ordinary wife, mother, and grandmother from Wellsville, Kansas (pop. 2026). She had no art background at all until, at age 68, she enrolled in one drawing course at a local university. The course focused on learning contour drawing—an extreme version of Nicolaïdes' dictum to "touch the model with your eyes."

Elizabeth's "model" was almost always herself, which she drew from her reflection in a mirror. Energized by that one class—she never took another—Elizabeth began a daily practice of self-portraiture using no other media than simple colored pencils. Like the Mexican artist Frida Kahlo, Layton excelled at distorting the self-portrait to reveal secret and often tormented inner states.

A key fact of Elizabeth's life story is that she had always suffered from crippling, chronic depression, which she powerfully depicted in her self-portraits. Amazingly, though, as she continued her daily drawing practice, her depression lifted and her self-portraits became softer and sometimes filled with joy, even as she examined, with unblinking honesty, her own deterioration due to increasing age. With these self-portraits Layton joined the ranks of so-called naïve artists with little or no art background who can sometimes create astounding bodies of work.

Eventually, Don Lambert, a newspaper reporter

from a nearby small town, "discovered" her work and made it his mission to introduce it to the world. He and Elizabeth made it their mission to let others know that art can be more than a mere decoration but can actually change lives.

To Elizabeth, art was a miracle, not a stepping stone to fame or profit. She was reportedly unconcerned about accolades for her work. She never attempted to sell her drawings but rather donated them to causes she cared about. Partly through Lambert's efforts, however, her drawings came to be exhibited in more than 200 museums and art centers across the country, including the Smithsonian, where I heard Lambert himself present them.

I am moved and chastened by Elizabeth's sense of art as a selfless pursuit. I, on the other hand, seem to be looking to art as a stairway to a new place in the sun—but isn't art the most flimsy vehicle imaginable to get me there?

My next brush with art school takes place at the University of the District of Columbia, a historically black college that primarily attracts students living in the District who can't afford the tuition elsewhere. Seniors like me who live here can also attend UDC free of charge. What have I got to lose? Everything looks promising as the class unfolds. Frankly, these up-and-coming students of color are a refreshing change from the leisured suburbanites in my classes at the Art League. The professor, Daniel, is passionate about teaching these students to draw. At every class session, he makes the rounds of the studio and stops at every easel, making pertinent comments as to how to improve each student's work. I can't help but admire the rapport he has—a white man who grew up in Richmond, Virginia—with these inner-city students.

Daniel also turns out to be a gifted artist, as I find out in an early class demonstration of how to measure the proportions of the figure accurately with nothing but a pencil. Focusing all his attention on the posed model in front of the class, Daniel sights across a pencil held at arm's length—not just once, but many times, tilting the pencil at various angles to measure the relationship of the limbs to the torso and the head. He then transfers each measurement to the paper, triangulat*ing* the measurements to ensure accuracy before drawing a light line. Gradually, an accurately proportioned rendering of the model begins to emerge on the paper.

Watching Daniel's virtuoso performance, I realize how sloppy I've been as a "winger" of proportions. Since I read Nicolaïdes' book, I have always pooh-poohed artists holding up a pencil at arm's length as a cliché, preferring to "eyeball" the image based on some kind of gestalt that I think I can organically perceive—but I often end up with too-short legs or other proportion mistakes. What Daniel is demonstrating is a form of structural anatomy, based on centuries-old techniques of depicting the human figure according to lessons passed down from Leonardo da Vinci and old masters who made rigorous studies of the human form. It's a necessary adjunct to Nicolaïdes' organic approach to drawing the figure and a crucial next step for me..

It seems I've hit the jackpot: this urban university turns out to have a superb art teacher. I want to learn all I can from Daniel, and I very much want him to affirm that I have talent and am on the right track in my late journey into art.

Trouble is, my presence in the class seems something of a nuisance for Daniel. As the semester wears on, he stops less and less often by my easel with advice and encouragement. It may simply be that, as a nonpaying student auditing the class, I make more work for him in an overcrowded classroom. Ultimately, though, I just keep plugging along, hoping to reverse this dynamic—after all, I do value Daniel's confirmation that I am really making progress in this art journey. But when I ask him to comment on the best drawing of a nude I've done in a long time, all I get is a curt "that's not bad."

When Nell Painter, the retired history professor of great acclaim, enrolled in the graduate art program at the Rhode Island School of Design, her adviser would regularly visit her studio to survey her progress. "You can't draw, and you can't paint," was the adviser's constant assessment. Yet Painter survived her criticism and went on to graduate from the program and even write a book about her experience, *Old in Art School.*

Daniel never lambasts my drawings the way Painter's adviser lambasted hers. My experience is more of frosty avoidance—and yes, I do come away from Daniel's studio having gained a far greater understanding of the proportions of the figure and how to render them. The harsher lesson is that my venture into art is not going to be a cakewalk, and I am far too eager for early affirmation. I will have to endure a long process of what they call "paying your dues" if I am going to make anything of this late journey into art.

As it happens, my latest journey into figure drawing isn't my only late-life passion. Another is the art of playing and singing American roots music such as bluegrass. I wish I could report that that learning curve is going to be less bruising to my creative self-esteem than Daniel's slights.

But no, another pummeling is in store for me next Monday evening, in a place called Hell's Bottom.

CHAPTER 4

Hell's Bottom

*We've one short life and, while we'll all look
differently at what it means to fully live that life
with no regrets, it is often the fear of risk that
stands in the way. Overcoming that fear gets us to a
place where we can more intentionally engage life,
become the people we long to be.*
—David duChemin

Before I pull open the heavy steel door, I've already
heard it: the clanging rolls of a banjo, the signature
sound of bluegrass music. Every time I hear that sound,
I get a sinking feeling in the pit of my stomach.

The feeling isn't about being chased by crazed moun-
taineers. It's about another kind of vulnerability. I'm a
beginner at this music, and I'm barging into a room full
of hot bluegrass players, or "pickers," as they prefer to
be called, who've been playing this music for decades.
Tonight, will I make an acceptable showing in the jam or
will I fall on my musical face?

A common denominator of many creative endeavors, I am finding, is risk. Discouraging as it may seem, there is no progress in many of the creative arts if you insist on staying in your comfort zone. This is particularly true of the arts in which there is some performance aspect—playing live music, singing, storytelling, acting. I could be trying to lead a song in a group of seasoned musicians and forgetting the words or, worse, singing off-key. But it's also true of non-performing arts. You could plow years of effort into writing a book, for example, only to find that no one wants to publish it, or if anyone does, hardly anyone wants to read it.

And yet the willingness to embrace risk, I am finding, is key to being creative at any age. William Sadler wrote that the older adults in his study "have determined where they want to go next in their lives and what really matters. But after looking within, they accept the risks of doing something different to realize a dream."

Still, "paying your dues" is part of the time-honored process of learning to play any kind of music. And bluegrass night at the Veterans of Foreign Wars (VFW) Post 350 in Takoma Park, Maryland, is advertised as an open jam, which means that anyone, beginner to pro, can join in. So, clutching the handle of my mandolin case tighter, I pull on that door, and the clattering rolls of the banjo push against me as I step inside.

VFW Post 350 is a windowless, concrete-block building in a neighborhood informally known as "Hell's Bottom," a low-lying, poorly drained area of fixer-upper homes in the otherwise prosperous suburb of Takoma Park, Maryland. The post has an atmosphere all its own—the stale and musty atmosphere of a windowless building that hasn't been aired out in decades. In years gone by, grizzled combat vets bellied up to the bar in the low-ceilinged room and nursed bargain-priced drinks. Nowadays you rarely see a vet—they have likely moved on to managed care facilities. With their departure, the VFW has found a new purpose as a venue for weekly jam sessions and performances of local musicians.

Almost everything here reeks of nostalgia, like the still-operational jukebox that you can play at no charge. You can still have a draft beer or a shot of whiskey for not much money. (The shots have been known to contain a dead fly.) The men's room has the obligatory male humor posted over the urinal: "Lean closer—it's shorter than you think." All in all, this place is the battered, beer-stained, timeworn Real Thing. It's hard not to feel a grudging affection for it.

So here I am at the VFW toting a budget mandolin. The risk I'm about to take may seem trivial—nothing more than embarrassing myself in public—but it still takes me way out of my comfort zone. The mandolin feels like a foreign object in my hands.

The pickers stand two deep around a scarred and battered old pool table set on a low stage. At the end of the table is Barb, a pretty but unsmiling woman with curly blond hair, on standup bass. The real person in charge of the group, though, is Ed, a slim older man with a white mustache who plays a Martin guitar and always wears a cap, even indoors. He's a stickler for the conventions of bluegrass, which has been described as a music that is less about what you can do than what you *can't* do.

But Ed is also a fine singer and a songwriter who leads his own band and has actually produced some good CDs. It's odd that he's not known outside the local bluegrass community, but then bluegrass is a niche music with room for only a few stars nationwide.

I'm getting to know some of the other pickers, about

a dozen in all this Monday night. There's Bobby, a tall, lanky transplant from Alabama, a physicist by day who plays banjo in the complex Earl Scruggs style by night; Alex, a North Carolina native and good mandolin player who works in publishing; Barry, a Columbia University graduate, now retired from the Labor Department, who also plays mandolin, but in a delicate cross picking style; and Lou, a small, smiling, bearded man and a fine fiddler who grew up in western Pennsylvania and now runs a graphic design business out of his home.

Most of the players at the VFW tonight lack any tangible connection with the kind of life that gave rise to this music. Few if any grew up on a farm, much less endured the kinds of rural privation that this music so eloquently expresses. Yet here we are, paying homage to a musical genre that connects us (or not) to an earlier time, to the lives of people living on remote, hardscrabble Appalachian farms, their lost loves, the grinding poverty that forced some to leave their mountain hollows for factory jobs in the city, and the broken-hearted nostalgia for what they left behind.

The jam session is a peculiar and very American institution. It's not a musical performance—there is almost never an audience to cater to. Nor is it intended as a rehearsal for some future performance. It's all about the love of this music and the challenge of playing to the utmost limit of your ability in real time. It's also a group experience that calls upon all your senses and motor skills to lock in with the rhythm, tempo, and chord progression of the other pickers. Players "woodshed" songs at home, memorizing lyrics and picking patterns to be ready for the jam, where they take turns in the challenging role of leading a song. When a jam is in full cry—especially when you are successfully sharing in or even leading a song—the energy can be exhilarating.

For many of the pickers at the VFW tonight, this music is right at the center of their lives. Many have years of lessons under their belts, and travel long distances to attend bluegrass festivals. Some of them, like Ed, are active in local bands. Their instruments may be worth thousands of dollars and are treated as revered craft objects. By contrast, I'm just learning to play this budget mandolin. It feels like a foreign object in my hands.

Being a greenhorn, right at the bottom of the ladder, is a status I haven't experienced in a while. When I was at the landscape magazine, I felt as though I was at the top of my game. Diving into the arts as an older adult, though, I'll be tackling a learning curve on which success is not assured. Along the way, I'll be blundering into situations where I'm starting at the bottom and working my way up. That would seem more doable if I were young and strong and ready to take on the world. Instead, I'm a retiree, gray haired and myopic, on a quest that calls for energy and a dash of bravado. I don't have a surplus of either. So what the hell am I doing in Hell's Bottom tonight?

Answer: I yearn to play music, period. Rather late in life, I discovered that music pulls up something from deep inside me that desperately needs to be heard. This is part of the quest that is drawing me forward: to find out whether someone well past his prime can thrive as a musician, where success is not guaranteed. But I'd better get comfortable taking chances if I ever want to find a place in the potentially transformative world of bluegrass.

My first earful of live bluegrass picking came one Sunday afternoon in a park in Arlington, Virginia, and what most struck me was its incongruity. The scene couldn't have been more bucolic: a circle of guitarists,

A note on the drawings in this book: All were sketched on the spot, from direct observation. No photographs or other artificial aids were used. (The one exception where a photo was used is my drawing of Neal Pattman, who died before I could sketch him.) The roughness of all the sketches is a direct result of drawing from life and is a part of my journey into seeing the world around me.

banjo players (of course) and other string players, about eight in all, gathered under a spreading ash tree. But this wasn't a hollow in the mountains. It was a park in a built-up Arlington, Virginia, a hotbed of technological innovation, crisscrossed by fiber optic cables and interstate highways.

I can't say I was crazy about the sound at first—the sewing-machine licks of the mandolin, the clanging rolls of the banjo, the keening wail of the fiddle. The breakneck tempo was new to me, as were the dense clusters of notes that seemed to pile one on top of the other, so different from the languid blues that were my first musical love. Granted, some of the pickers were really good at what they did, playing really fast single-note lines or holding down a rock-steady rhythm on a host of standards that they had obviously learned by ear and could play note for note, in a host of intricate variations.

As I drew closer to the circle, I realized that the pickers didn't just seem to be from another place. With their acoustic instruments and old-timey songs, they were throwbacks to another time—a rural America of small family farms where families gathered around a floor-model radio console in the evening and, on Sundays, sang gospel songs in close harmony in that old country church down the road.

Washington, D.C. and its suburbs, I would soon find, is bluegrass country, with a slew of local bands and regular jam sessions like this one. In fact, Washington has been called the Bluegrass Capital of the World, partly because its nearness to the Blue Ridge Mountains where this music was born. Regular jam sessions such as the one at the VFW have been running for years. On any given week, pickers who love this music can take part in more jam sessions in this area than in any other place in the country.

As it happens, I have a lost connection to the culture that gave birth to this music. I've noted earlier in these pages that my family on both sides came out of the Blue Ridge Mountains, the descendants of Scots-Irish settlers who gravitated to those mountains even before the American Revolution and who established farms on those steep, rocky ridges.

Theirs was a life of isolation and hardship. As a child in a remote mountain valley in the Blue Ridge, my maternal grandmother was bitten by a copperhead. She lingered for days between life and death as her immune system battled the poison. Obviously, she survived. Those people were tough.

My grandfather came from several ridges over but established himself as a veterinarian in Walhalla, then a trading town at the foot of those mountains. When my grandmother's family traveled down from their Blue Ridge farm to buy supplies, my grandfather first saw her, a mountain beauty sitting upright on the seat of the family buggy.

When my brother, Bolling, was a boy in the 1950s, our Uncle Frank took him to our grandfather's birthplace, a "God-forsaken place on the side of the mountain," as Bolling recounts it. "Hard to imagine farming in such a place. All seemed on a slant." The family who now owned the land lived in a rough cabin and spoke with such a thick mountain accent that Bolling could hardly understand them. By way of hospitality, a boy about twelve milked the family cow and offered the visitors a drink of the warm unfiltered milk.

The music my mountain forbears played was the direct ancestor of the bluegrass music we play every Monday at the VFW. This music was adapted from the fiddle tunes they brought over from Scotland and Ireland with the addition of a new instrument, the African-American banjo. By the time my mother and father were born, though, their families had migrated to towns and found the roughshod music of the hills outdated and hokey. So it's not surprising that my first earful of bluegrass sounded alien to me. The raw, archaic sound of this music was part of a culture my family had long since left behind. The question is: Do I really want to forge that link anew?

Tonight at the VFW, Ed calls the first song, Norman Blake's "Last Train from Poor Valley," a moving lament of unemployment and lost love in Appalachia. Bobby kicks off the melody on the banjo—a cluster of finger-picked notes that seem to tumble over one another in a frantic but precise rhythm while the mandolin players chop out a percussive backbeat that sounds something like a snare drum (real drums are taboo in bluegrass—another of the "can't dos" of this music), while Barb's upright bass calls out a clippity-clop rhythm. Most of the players keep looking down at their hands, making sure their fingers

are in the right places so they can rigorously stay with the chord changes. Everyone is in high spirits, but this jam is not a place where you have a few drinks and just "play what you feel." You are here to call up the spirits of the ancestors—the great early bluegrass bands.

Ed sings out the first verse, his fine tenor voice carrying the melody of the song as I struggle to stay on the offbeat groove with Alex and Barry. Like most white people, I instinctively clap on the downbeat and am always in danger of transferring that habit to the mandolin, which would muddle the sound of the ensemble and bring immediate cries of approbation down on me. But tonight I listen hard to the others and strive to match their split-second timing. It will take a long time to internalize the offbeat timing of the mandolin chop, but tonight I manage to stay in lock step. Little else in my life has been such a model of coordination and mutual support in real time where the slightest mistake would be glaringly obvious.

Now the instrumental breaks begin to make their way around the pool table. The most striking aspect of a bluegrass jam, which bluegrass founder Bill Monroe borrowed from jazz, is the "break" or improvised solo. At the VFW, the solos move clockwise around the pool table, and each player gets a chance to shine for the space of a full song verse. Competent soloists—"hot pickers"—are the stars of the jam, and their solos can turn into complex improvisations over the simple chord progression. Clumsy pickers are very low on the totem pole, but each gets to shine for the space of a song verse—or stumble in full view of everyone.

Most of the pickers seem to know the lyrics and chords of the songs by heart. They also know intuitively when the picker ahead of them has finished his brief solo and when it's their turn. This kind of intuitive understanding is what makes any bluegrass jam hang together. When it's Ed's turn, the fingers of his left hand snake deftly up and down the fretboard of his Martin guitar while his right hand picks out a solo that transforms the melody of the song into something fresh and spontaneous—and so much of the moment that it cannot be repeated. Then Lou bows a wailing fiddle solo with his eyes closed and his torso gently swaying.

"Don't slow down," calls out Barb, and I wonder if I'm the one causing the rhythm to drag.

Then it's my turn to solo, and the old sinking feeling sinks deeper. Will I be able to pick a reasonable mandolin solo, or will my fingers tense up, making me lose the rhythm or even play a wrong note? As the fingers of my left hand move over the cuttingly thin mandolin strings, my right hand clutches the pick, searching for those elusive notes. The plucked notes come out sounding more like chopsticks than a fluid mandolin solo, but the other pickers are looking down at their instruments, seeming oblivious to my discomfiture.

Oddly enough, a solution to my clumsiness is sitting on the pool table in front of me: a set of harmonicas in the typical keys used in bluegrass, packed in a battered tin that once held Turkish toffee. I've been playing this humble instrument—colloquially known as the "harp" or "tin sandwich"—for thirty plus years, inspired by a one-armed black man I met in my native Georgia; he sang and played with eloquence and passion. When I moved to Houston, Texas, I cut my teeth playing the blues and country-western music behind a couple of singer/guitarists at open mikes in sweaty beer joints, where I was paid in cold beer and found out that a wailing, tuneful harmonica solo could command applause from appreciative Texans.

But playing harmonica is, in many jams, another of the unwritten taboos of bluegrass. Bill Monroe, who founded this music, decreed five "bluegrass instruments" that were common in the old time American string bands. If you play any instrument outside those five, you risk immediate rejection. Tonight at the VFW, I leave the harmonicas in their Turkish toffee tin.

Ed concludes the song with a final chorus, and those who grasp the mysterious art of vocal harmony mirror the melancholy last lines. Then the song is over, and smiles of satisfaction crease the faces of some of the other musicians. All I've done is made it through another song.

My turn to lead a song. Why does this feel like a moment of truth?

It all goes back to running that small risk—and, like many older adults, I tend to shy away from anything that gets me out of my comfort zone. Take singing: I've never done much of it outside the shower, so the idea of leading a song in this jam—and possibly embarrassing myself in full view of everyone around the pool table—is scary. But I know that if I want to sing—and, like most people, I've always wanted to—I have to take that step sometime. Choking down my self-doubt, I choose the old Stanley Brothers mournful query, "Who Will Sing for Me?"

I launch into the song with an uneasy strum, unsure that my right hand will "chop" on those mandatory off-beats. Tonight, though, I seem to passing that test—my chops sound in time with the other mandolin players—but will my voice betray my lack of confidence as I pre-pare to lead the song?

Still, I launch into the mournful first verse:

Oft I sing for my friends
When death's cold hand I see
When I reach my journey's end
Who will sing one song for me?

Then the chorus:
Who will sing—

Ed stops me cold—"That's not how it goes!"—and all the instruments freeze into a deadly silence.

Hot shame flushes my face. Stopping a singer in mid verse is unheard of, a brutal vote of no confidence in front of everybody. What Ed is really telling me is: You're not worthy to play with us.

"You can sing the chorus any way you want to." Ed says amid the frozen silence, "but that's not the way the chorus starts." He confidently sings the correct first line:

"I wonder who ... will sing ... for me ...."

My memory brutally jogged, I somehow find my way back to the approved lyrics and manage to resume singing—but weakly and hesitantly, my breathing hollowed out. Somehow I manage to finish the last verse, and it's over—pitifully over.

I manage to make it through the rest of the evening, but feel gutted, mortified. If this is what they call "paying your dues," do I really want to be singled out for an extra-whopping dose of them?

Never, ever stay in a musical or other performance situation where you are disrespected. That is a rule I will forge for myself going forward. If I follow that rule tonight, I ought to walk out of the heavy steel door right now and never return—and I'd be right. On the other hand, I'd be closing the door to bluegrass forever behind me.

Bottom line: I desperately want to play music. And for better or for worse, I'm living in bluegrass country. So two weeks from now, I'll be back again for bluegrass night at the VFW. Still, how strange it is to be here tonight, a rank beginner in this music, at the very bottom of the pecking order. But honestly, I'm not trying so much to find a musical home in Hell's Bottom as to recreate a musical home that I left behind in faraway Houston. There, years ago, I had many happier evenings of music under the moniker of Atlanta Bill, the kick-ass harmonica player, at a place called the Ice House.

CHAPTER 5

Becoming Atlanta Bill

Athens, Georgia circa 1979

From inside the basement of the university cafeteria came the sound of someone singing in a deep baritone voice, interspersed with a wailing, or crying sound, that was almost human. Pulled by the music and singing, I came to a room where stood a powerfully built, middle-aged Black man. He had only one arm, and with his one good hand he was holding a cheap ten-hole harmonica up to his mouth. He was the reason I'd come here, having heard that there was a cafeteria worker who played a mean harp. And sure enough, from the tiny instrument he coaxed the haunting sounds of a music that seemed exotic and yet eerily familiar. If you're imagining a pasty-faced harmonica rendition of "O Susannah" played around a campfire, this was something totally different. This was primitive, this was simplistic, but it was deep. It chugged. It wailed. It exactly complemented the man's deep, tuneful singing voice.

The big man was Neal Pattman, and the place was the University of Georgia campus, where I had recently enrolled in the landscape architecture program that would eventually lead to my career at the magazine. In fact, I'd never really played or sung anything, at least not expecting that anyone would want to hear it. But I recently discovered a burning desire to make music, any music, and that yearning led me to the basement of the university cafeteria.

There are those rare moments in life when our free will, our power to choose between this, that, and the other, is annulled and we are in the grip of an impulse more powerful than our own conscious choice. This was one of those moments. The first time I listened to Pattman, I knew I had to learn to play this earthy, no-frills music, whatever it took.

Neal Pattman was part of the rural tradition of playing unaccompanied blues harmonica—that is, playing rhythm and melody without a guitarist to back up this simplest of instruments.

Unaccompanied harmonica is the sound of loneliness, a sound that grew out of rural deprivation in the South, out of the kinds of lives that longed for expression, and sometimes the only outlet within reach was the cheap ten-hole harmonica. Some of the most prominent exemplars of the style were further hampered, like Pattman, by physical disabilities. (Pattman lost his right arm in an accident involving a wagon wheel at the age of seven.)

One of the most renowned was Sonny Terry, who lost his eyesight as a child but taught himself a powerful style of unaccompanied harmonica that mixed wailing bent notes with chugging rhythm chords and seamless vocal lines punctuated by wild whoops and hollers.

Terry eventually became famous and toured the world with guitarist Brownie McGhee.

DeFord Bailey, another disabled player, was stricken with polio as child and never grew taller than four feet ten. His only school of music was the nearby train trestle, where he would stand and emulate the rushing sound of the locomotive, thereby cultivating an impeccable sense of rhythm. At the height of his career, Bailey regularly performed at the Grand Ole Opry, where he stood alone on the stage and held white audiences spellbound with his playing that sounded like two or three harmonicas playing at once.

Pattman was part of that musical lineage. A local harmonica player taught him the basics of "blowing harp" and introduced him to the trade of playing for neighbors at rural dances and breakdown parties. He later sang and played unaccompanied harmonica for tips on the streets of the college town of Athens. Eventually, Pattman was to enjoy a modest brush with fame. In 1989, he took his down-home blues to New York City, where he'd been invited to play at in a blues show at Lincoln Center. As a result of that engagement, he began to be booked at festivals, went on a 48-city tour with nationally famous artist Taj Mahal, and even traveled to England to play at London's 100 Club. He recorded a few albums of his own music, such as *The Blues Ain't Left Yet,* which are still available, although he never became known outside the small circle of acoustic blues fans. He died in 2005.

It's uncanny how impulses that permanently change our lives can break through at a time when our settled life lurches off the rails. I'm not talking about passing fancies or hobbies that come and go. I'm talking about life-changing passions that persist for years or even the rest of your days. My fascination with the blues began in that cafeteria basement in my late thirties and, forty years later, I am even more fascinated than I was then, even though the African American experience that gave rise to this music will always be foreign to me. Still, at that point in my life I was suffering my own white man's blues, for which this music would become the perfect expression and, just possibly, part of the cure.

A few years earlier, my life had lurched off the rails. On the surface, everything seemed to be chugging along extremely well. I was in my late thirties and living in New York City with a steady job teaching remedial reading to adults at one of the city universities. I was married to my first wife, Helen, and we had two beautiful young children, Emily and Chris. We enjoyed a spacious two-bedroom apartment on the Upper West Side of Manhattan. So yes, everything seemed in apple-pie order.

I'd met Helen at a poetry reading in Greenwich Village in the late sixties. She was an openhearted Englishwoman with alabaster skin and the sweetest expression I had ever set eyes on. We quickly found we had many interests in common—writing, the arts, yoga—as well as an immediate physical sympathy. By the time we met at that poetry reading, marriage and children were foreordained.

As I got to know Helen better, I discovered a delicate, high-strung, dreamy woman with little interest in practical life decisions. We were soul mates--both extreme introverts with counterculture leanings and artistic aspirations. If marriages tend to succeed where there is a balance of complementary traits and inclinations, the very closeness of our natures portended our marriage's demise.

Even more pressing was a career issue. I detested my job. I'd spent many years teaching remedial reading to adults, a role I'd fallen into because I had a couple of degrees in English, not because I had any real interest in bringing underserved adults up to speed. The students deserved a more caring, committed teacher, and I couldn't be that for them. I've often heard that one can learn to love almost any job—it's all a matter of attitude. That has never worked for me. If the job doesn't suit me,

I am constitutionally incapable to convincing my heart that it does.

One cold winter, Helen and I packed up the kids and boarded a train to Charleston, South Carolina, to find some sunshine. Charleston in the 1970s was not the glittering resort destination it is today. It was a decaying bastion of Southern gentility that appeared to be still recovering from Reconstruction. For me, it was love at first sight—the historic city with its stately buildings and narrow, winding streets, the vast expanses of salt marsh and ocean, the live oaks draped with Spanish moss, the sense of history.

I interviewed and quickly found a comparable position at the local technical college. Everything seemed to be falling into place. What I didn't understand was that the move to Charleston was a cover-up for evading deeper issues in my life. What had seemed an opening into a bright new phase of life was actually a dead end. As for Charleston itself, after the infatuation wore off I found it a very aloof, standoffish city where friends were hard to come by. The few I met came via the sport of road bicycling. Other than the time I spent with my kids, my main joys were fast rides on the flat rural roads around Charleston, where the salt marshes, live oak hummocks, lush bird life, and wide, slow-moving rivers intensified an existing interest in the configuration and ecology of landscapes.

At the technical college my lukewarm interest in teaching remedial reading to adults degenerated almost into outright loathing. Many of the students, who received a government stipend to attend classes, seemed more interested in the stipend than in actually learning anything. As my lack of interest in the program became more obvious to my supervisor, one day I found myself on the street, which in some ways was a great relief. Now I could begin the difficult process, in my late thirties, of casting about for a career path I could love—if not a career that involved writing, at least something more suited to my interests than teaching remedial reading.

My separation from Helen was a little more complicated, but like good soulmates we parted with remarkably little rancor and were able to share parental visits over the next few years, though I will confess that the burden of parenting fell mostly on Helen. I left our car with her and walked away from the life we shared almost empty-handed—no TV, no electronics, not much else in the world, just my clothes, a few books, and my beloved bicycle. Fortunately, I had a few friends in a nearby ashram where I regularly practiced yoga poses. This big old house had an attic space vacant, where I deposited my few possessions and basically camped out. In this void between careers, I had assumed the role of a rootless wanderer who seemed to have taken a vow of poverty.

It wasn't supposed to turn out this way, so different from the expectations of the world in which I'd grown up. The son of an Atlanta pediatrician, I came from a graceful neighborhood of spacious homes with sweeping lawns. The land behind our house was designed by a landscape architect and featured massive stone steps leading down to a stone bridge over a native stream, beyond which were formal planting beds. My mother was trained as a public health nurse, but Dad's practice was successful enough that she could stay at home and raise me and my brother, Bolling, and devote her free time to elite women's clubs. In short, my entire childhood and youth had been all about financial security, privilege, and the expectation of upward mobility. Living in a rented room over an ashram, unemployed, was one of the most unlikely outcomes my parents could have imagined—or that I could easily come to terms with. I was stuck, unable to envision my next way forward.

It should come as no surprise, then, that the master's program in landscape architecture at the University of Georgia beckoned like a lighthouse to a lost sailor. As I prepared to relocate to Athens, I hatched the radical idea of relocating via my ten-speed bicycle. Somehow, the nomadic simplicity of the long road journey was a powerful and necessary symbol of my leaving one failed life behind and journeying, footloose and low-tech, toward a new, uncertain destiny. So I loaded the panniers with the bare essentials and set off for the three-day journey across the flat roads of the South Carolina Low Country and on to the rolling red-clay hills of northeast Georgia. I slept in fields by the side of the highway.

What I thought was a new beginning when I pedaled into Athens was, however, the definitive end of my life as I had known it. The middle-class comfort I had grown up with became an even more distant memory as I embraced the monkish lifestyle of an impoverished graduate student. I didn't even have a guarantee of financing; I'd have to supplement a small scholarship with menial landscape work. I was lucky enough to get a free room in an old house in exchange for tending the yard. My sparse possessions became even sparser—I didn't even own a radio.

One of the surprises to emerge from this self-imposed state of disintegration was this yearning to express myself in music. I have no idea what sparked that particular creative urge. Although I'd tested high in music aptitude in elementary school, I refused to take part in school bands. This seemingly sudden interest in music in my late thirties probably had something to do, paradoxically, with my settled life coming apart.

With no experience in school band or anything else related to music, the only instrument that seemed accessible was the humble ten-hole harmonica. Like most people who pick up the tiny instrument, I had taught myself a couple of simple folk songs (think "Red River Valley"). But these tepid numbers did nothing to answer the creative urge that was boiling up inside me.

The educator John Holt, in his 1978 book, *Never Too Late: My Musical Life Story,* expressed a high-minded aim for the monumental challenge of taking up the cello in middle age. "If I could learn to play the cello well, as I thought I could, I could show by my own example that we all have greater powers than we think; that whatever we want to learn or learn to do, we probably can learn; that our lives and our possibilities are not determined by what experts say we can or cannot do. . . . .To many people, music now seems an unapproachable mystery. I hoped to find ways to make it something that all who wanted might take part in for themselves."

Much as I admire Holt's altruism, I must admit that I had no such fine motivations. Instead, I had a burning desire to find my sound, to sing my song, the song that I sensed I was meant to sing. I didn't care if the music was simple or complex, as long as it came straight from the heart--or maybe from the gut. Straight from the fires of creation.

But I needed a catalyst that could unlock the music inside me. Could Neal Pattman's simple, earthy blues be that catalyst? And could I mimic the old archetype of the young urban white guy learning to play the blues from an older rural Black man? (Except, of course, that I wasn't that young.)

The harmonica is such a deceptive instrument. As

actor/musician Hugh Laurie put it, "Generally speaking, musical instruments are easier to play than they look—with the exception of the harmonica. You pick one up, and you think, 'How hard can it be?'"

I quickly found out how hard, if you want to play real music on it—and by music I mean actual tunes played note-for-note with a clear, singing tone. I'm not talking about emulating the off-key huffing and puffing of some folk and rock stars. (Think Bob Dylan.) The harmonica is truly "the blind man's instrument"—you can't see anything you're doing, so you're feeling your way across the tiny mouthpiece with your lips. Then, to produce a clear single note, you have to pucker up, try to find the place where that note you need is located, and figure out whether you need to suck or blow it. (If you guess wrong it's a disaster.) Worse, the note layout is confusing. Two notes of the scale are missing in the low register, and then the sequence of notes reverses at hole seven. All this confusion on a tiny instrument with a total of only twenty notes.

Pattman drove up to my apartment in his big old Oldsmobile. It was my first music lesson, ever. Pattman settled on my dilapidated couch and fished a shiny B-flat harmonica out of his pocket. He had a wonderful gentleness of speech and manner that belied his physical strength. (Even with only one arm, he worked for a time as a bouncer in a local, black night club.)

The lesson was not a notable success, however. Like many intuitive musicians, Pattman couldn't put into words what he was physically doing when he played, much less break it down into easy steps for a beginner to follow.

"Here, play this," he said, and played a fragment of a tune that, to him, must have seemed childishly simple.

But without any guidance as to how to shape my mouth cavity or when to blow and when to draw and into what hole, it seemed impossibly difficult to reproduce those sounds on my own harmonica—and, worse, I didn't know what questions to ask. So although Neal Pattman was to remain my lifelong inspiration, I didn't ask for a second lesson.

My musical journey should rightfully have ended after my first failed lesson with Pattman. But then I heard about an instruction book and three audio cassettes that I could get by mail order from Jon Gindick, a harmonica teacher in California. I mailed a check and waited expectantly for the postman.

Life-changing guidance can come from the most humble and unexpected places, Billed as the absolute basic beginner's guide to blues harmonica, the book consisted of a folksy text and cartoonish diagrams. How strange to be in graduate school at a university and simultaneously starting a romper-room course in music instruction. It was incongruous. It was infantile. It was perfect. Gindick's bare-bones instructions turned out to be the key that literally opened the world of music to me.

On the cheap audio cassettes (yes, these were the seventies), Gindick demonstrated the sounds diagrammed in the book and then played a chord progression on his guitar so that one could practice the riffs and sounds with backup. The first lesson showed how to pucker the lips to play a clear single note, the essential first step of playing the harmonica. And what a thrill to blow that first, round, beautiful hornlike note!

The higher hill to climb was the technique of "bending" or distorting notes to produce the wailing sound characteristic of the blues. With my lips closed around the mouthpiece, the diagram directed me to make my mouth cavity as large and loose as possible while contorting my tongue as I drew a deep breath. With that,

the brass reeds of the harmonica began to sing—but if it was a song it was a ragged, distorted, heartbroken one that seemed utterly alien to be coming out of my indrawn breath. I didn't know I had such a sound inside me, but here it was for all the world to hear. Voicing that cry of yearning and sorrow pulled up something from deep inside me that was just starting to find its voice. The sound carried, though, and the energy I put into my daily practice drew varying responses from neighbors. "That's a mean note!" said one by way of compliment, while another loudly slammed a door each time I started to wail. Still, I persisted.

Gindick's approach confirmed my predilection for self-teaching. This is probably rooted in my contrarian nature, my stubborn tendency to hack out my own path—doubtless a roundabout way of learning, rife with dead ends, but it's my way. I could hardly have guessed, from that more-than-humble musical beginning, what a long and convoluted path I had set my foot on. It would mean decades of searching down blind alleys looking for a musical home and finding, along the way, isolated moments of transcendent joy.

An odd sidebar to my learning harmonica: My son, Chris, was learning guitar at the same time.

Helen had moved the kids out of her second-floor apartment in downtown Charleston to a barrier island south of the city, where she had bought a cheaply built ranch-style home on a scruffy rural road that led down to a fishing pier. Johns Island was, in the 1970s, a rural backwater that hadn't yet made the transition to a fashionable, farther-out suburb of Charleston. It was the South at its most rural, where the next-door neighbors dumped their broken plumbing fixtures in their back yard and a rattlesnake made its nest in Helen's garage.

What a strange outpost she'd come to—a fresh-faced English girl who'd emigrated to New York full of dreams and expectations and had somehow ended up, a single mom with two kids, on this dead-end road leading to a salt marsh.

But Helen was struggling to turn her love of painting into a livelihood. During the 1990s she would transition out of her job as a medical assistant and gradually carve out a modest niche in the Charleston art scene. The main theme of her bold, colorful canvases was the physical love between man and woman, and what she lacked in technique and finesse Helen made up with in-your-face emotion. In time, she made a modest living with her art, an achievement that continues to command my total admiration. Much of her modest income came from direct sales from a stall in the colonnaded public market downtown.

My kids' childhoods, then, were tightly bound to the isolation of the barrier island, where they were two city kids with no one like them living anywhere nearby. When they went into Charleston each day, they would attend inner-city schools and always be at a disadvantage among the children of the local elite. As the children of a struggling painter and an even more struggling graduate student, they would never, throughout their growing years, experience the privilege and economic security I had known as the son of a doctor in Atlanta.

Chris responded by turning inward, and turning to the guitar. Immersing himself in music was a way of dealing with the boredom and isolation on the barrier island where he knew absolutely no one. Helen bought him a cheap Harmony electric that too frequently went out of tune and a small amplifier. He locked himself in his room and practiced for hours every day, focusing on

pentatonic scales, licks, and songs he learned from tab-
lature in *Guitar* magazine. He practiced so intently that
he wore down the steel frets on the Harmony. Finding
release in the lonely hours of practice set a pattern of solitary pursuits--fishing, sailboarding, and, of course, daily
guitar practice—that he follows these decades later.

I bought Chris his first acoustic guitar as a Christmas present. We went down to George's Loans & Music,
a pawn shop on King Street where Chris picked out a
good second-hand Fender and I forked over $254, which
was a lot of money for a monkish graduate student. (I
know the amount because, amazingly, Chris has kept the
receipt to this day.) An art buff at his high school painted
his guitar case with colorful Grateful Dead-type imagery.

The strange and sad part was that when I visited
from Athens and we saw one another, music, which

might have been a bridge to bring us closer, wasn't part of our picture. Some of the issue was that my traditional blues didn't necessarily jibe with his progressive rock, but that gulf could have been bridged if the will had been there. The core problem was that I was a mostly absentee father and he the son who surely resented me for not being a father in any conventional sense of the term. There was a wall between us that music couldn't yet breach.

At the same time that I was learning the simplest of instruments, Helen was attempting a far more ambitious musical project, taking up classical violin as she approached her fortieth birthday. She was already a decent recorder player, but this was not enough—she wanted to scale the heights of music and play in a local orchestra. I know she took some violin lessons; I'm not sure how rigorously she practiced or how much mental effort she put into understanding the nuances of technique required to play the violin. When I visited the kids she allowed me to stay in her house, where I was a captive audience as she practiced her scales and études. To my ears, these resembled a fingernail scratching down a blackboard. (Any reader who has lived with a violin student may recognize that excruciating sound.)

For an adult to pick up a new instrument and tackle the rigors of classical music as Helen did is, of course, possible. But anyone who attempts this must realize at the outset that they face years of rigorous lessons and practice—and that middle-aged reflexes are not ideally suited to the nuanced, tiny, fast-paced movements required to play an instrument well. Whether Helen even really understood the magnitude of the challenge she'd taken on, I don't know.

One day, I made the tactical mistake of asking Helen

what feedback she was hearing on her progress. Was her violin teacher or anyone else encouraging her to press on with her ambition to play in an orchestra? She bridled.

"Don't ever let anyone else set your course for you, Bill," she said. "You should always be sure in your heart of what you want to do—and do it."

Boy, does that sound arrogant, I thought but said nothing. Yet despite Helen's apparent self-assurance, after a couple of years it sank in that her playing was not getting noticeably better. She laid down her violin forever. Even sadder, she didn't pick up her recorder again.

Helen might have profited from reading *Never Too Late*. Holt took up the cello in middle age—cello being a really challenging instrument to take up as an adult— and aspired to play full-blown classical pieces on it, which is equally difficult to do. Holt tells in excruciating detail about the struggles to become even a minimally competent classical cellist. He practiced three to four hours a day, sacrificing other joys in his life such as visiting longtime friends, in order to take part in local orchestral gatherings of other amateur classical players, most of whom seemed to be much further advanced than he was. Holt recounts with admirable frankness how he was often so far behind the other players that he just packed up his cello and beat a retreat.

Reading Holt, I am torn between admiring his dedication to music and pity at his relative lack of success. Overall, his book is a cautionary tale about the risks of devoting one's life to any art form and to the dogged and almost heroic pursuit of craft that art requires.

So I plowed ahead teaching myself blues harmonica. A critical reader might point out that I set myself a mighty low bar—who couldn't learn to play the tin sandwich? Again, I respond that I don't mean making the harmonica squalls of the aforementioned rock stars or the warble of cub scouts sitting around a campfire. I wanted to extract a clear, singing tone out of the tiny instrument, to play actual tunes, note for note, and, if I played a blues riff or tune, I wanted to make the sad blue notes sound sweet and heartbreaking. If those are your goals, learning to play the harmonica is by no means easy.

It now seems, though, that I may have followed Helen's advice. Whatever anyone may think of my music (or, for that matter, my artwork or writing) I've set my own course, and I've followed what was in my heart—and been willing (mostly) to pay the price for following it.

We sat on folding chairs in a big circle, twenty or so of us facing one another, in the main hall of a community center in Houston. Most clasped guitars or other instruments, ready to play. I clasped my ten-hole harmonica. A sweet tension was in the air as each of us waited his turn to sing or play.

By now, I'd earned my master's degree in environmental design and was gainfully employed for the first time since I'd gone to graduate school, planning parking and pedestrian areas for the heavy-rail transit system under development in Houston. I'd rented a small apartment in Houston's Museum District. I'd begun casting about for musical opportunities and here I was, at the local folklore society's monthly song swap.

This was one of many of my life's crossroads moments. I'd been devotedly practicing for more than a year, and I was learning to play, not only down-home blues, but folk melodies note-for-note with sweeter and sweeter tone. Still, I'd never actually played in front of a live audience. If I delivered my song at least passably, I could move forward to explore the wonderful world of music, possibly sharing the gift of music with others. If I stumbled and fell flat on my face, I would be mortified in front of every person in that room, and I'd retreat to the role of the lonely harmonica player wailing out the blues in his back bedroom.

First up to sing was David Jones, a tall, bearded Texan and a powerful singer who delivered a song about heartbreak and lost love accompanied by his fine finger-picking on his steel-string guitar. Other musicians and would-be musicians followed. Then came the moment of truth for me.

I leaned forward in my chair, raised the harmonica to my lips, and blew the melodic riff that began the old spiritual, "Swing Low, Sweet Chariot." I played the great old melody note-for-note, alternated with snatches of singing the lyrics (weakly and timidly, given my complete lack of experience singing). After a couple of verses I stretched out into bluesy variations on the tune and. when I played a closing flourish—people clapped!

At the end of the evening we mingled, and I garnered compliments for my "bluesy" sound. Then David Jones approached me. "Nice harp playing," he said. "The singing wasn't much, but I like your harp work. I play at open mikes around town. Would you like to play behind me sometime? It'd be fun!"

Would I ever! In that moment, David's invitation catapulted me from practicing blues riffs in my bedroom to being a sideman to an accomplished local singer and guitarist. I was, it seemed, on my way into this expansive world of sound.

My debut as a musical sideman came one weekday evening at a local Ice House, a holdover from the days before air conditioning when ice making companies were fronted by open-air taverns where thirsty Texans could enjoy an ice-cold beer during Houston's steamy summers. We stood on a low stage facing a bar and roomful of tables packed with chattering beer drinkers.

When David leaned to the microphone and began picking his guitar, the chattering tapered off. When he sang out the first line of "The Midnight Special," I responded with a few bluesy fill notes. David leaned closer to the mike and told the story of the Black man condemned to work the prison farm in the sugarcane fields south of Houston and the yearning inspired by the train that passed at midnight, its headlight representing his lost freedom.

> *Let the Midnight Special shine a light on me*
> *Let the Midnight Special shine an ever-lovin' light*
> *on me*

As David sang his way through each sad verse, I held a single long note as he sang or filled in the empty spaces with more bluesy licks. Then David gave me a significant look, which signaled that this was my chance to step up to the mike and play lead against his guitar chords for the length of a verse.

As I drew a long breath into the harmonica, the brass reeds responded with a sweet and tuneful sound. I closed my eyes and drew an even stronger breath as I distorted my mouth cavity the way the diagram in Gindick's book had shown me. The brass tines of the harmonica began to sing out, somehow transforming a prisoner's heartbreak into a bittersweet lament.

> *Let the Midnight Special shine a light on me*

When I drew the last note of my solo, Lord have mercy! the room erupted into applause. I literally staggered back from the microphone in shock and delight. The song wasn't even over yet, and they were applauding for me! For me!

It would not be an exaggeration to say that my soul took wing in this moment. So much seemed to converge: my first earful of Neal Pattman's blues, the lonely hours of self-teaching, the sound of a door slammed when I wailed a note, the unlikely miracle of my making any music at all. In that grubby Ice House, for the first time since I'd taken up music, I finally understood what it meant to dance in the fires of creation.

As we were stepping down from the low stage, David finally introduced me. "This is Bill Thompson. This is his first time playing at the Ice House, and he doesn't know yet that he's good."

Many other great nights followed on that same low stage, and there were many more spontaneous rounds of applause for my harmonica solos. And then one night as I was enjoying a cold draft beer (the payoff for open mike musicians), a rawboned Texan with a scruffy red beard sidled up to the bar next to me.

Mike Hodges was a dogcatcher for the county. He'd grown up brawling and driving the back roads of Harris County, north of Houston, in his pickup truck. He looked tough. He was. He'd done a stint working in the oil fields before settling on animal control. And, like most Texans, he liked guns. A pistol was never far from his person.

I'd just heard him sing a song in a nasal country/ western vein at the open mike, accompanied only by his guitar. "Good job," I said. "So you're mainly a singer?"

"I'm mainly a writer," he said, meaning he wrote songs. "That was one of my own songs. Say, would you be interested in backing me up on harp sometime?" And so began my unlikely friendship with Mike Hodges. In the Atlanta I'd grown up in—a world of manicured lawns, degrees from Southern universities, and country club memberships—I would probably never even have met Mike, much less palled around with him. But that's homegrown music for you—it can ride roughshod over the niceties of social background.

Soon thereafter I drove north of Houston to Mike's house for a practice session. Following that, Mike gave me a tour of his rural neighborhood with its wide-open skies —the end of the woods, he called it—and we stopped in at a friend's house for drinks. This wasn't the kind of house I associated with oil-rich Texas. I stepped into a cube of four concrete-block walls sitting atop a dirt floor. In Houston, the most air-conditioned city in the country, this house had only an electric fan that barely moved the tepid air around the room. Still, drinking from a jug of cheap wine on that dirt floor was, for me, a key to appreciating the rural South where the soulful beauty of country music—the white man's blues—was born.

Then came the night at a local community center where we performed a set for a paying audience and Mike christened me with a new moniker. When the final applause died down, Mike said, "Please give a hand just to my friend here, Atlanta Bill Thompson."

Whoa! Suddenly I had a musical identity. I wasn't just a wage earner living in a one-bedroom apartment in downtown Houston. I was Atlanta Bill, the kick-ass harmonica player. The name stuck. It seemed I'd found, at the age of forty, a talent and a new expression of self I hadn't the slightest idea was in me.

A lifelong introvert, I began to be invited to parties and even acquired a steady girlfriend. I went from being a loner and a wallflower to being fairly popular. Through my musical connections, I even got to play harmonica on a couple of local recording dates. Playing harmonica for a radio commercial for a shoe chain in Oklahoma earned me just twenty dollars and a cassette tape of the recording session, but it yielded an enormous boost in confidence, which is absolutely key to any musician who aspires to play in front of others.

But always, it was the thrill of blowing those harmonica fills and solos to the applause of a live audience that drew me on. My cheap harp wailing across the beery atmosphere of the Ice House week after week dependably lifted me out of myself with moments of pure joy. Those moments became a touchstone of my entire life from then on. I thought they would never end.

How wrong I was. All too soon, the transit project was voted out of existence, and I was left high and dry in Texas with not much to fall back on. Suddenly family became tantamount to survival, and family was back in South Carolina. So I crammed all my worldly goods into my old Ford Maverick and headed out toward that little dead-end town, Walhalla, where my family would at least keep a roof over my head. Home, as Robert Frost put it, is where, when you have to go there, they have to take you in.

But what about my newly discovered talent as a kick-ass harmonica player? That was a talent I could carry with me as easily as a box of harmonicas, right? What I didn't understand, though, was how deeply my musical identity was rooted in this place, this hot, sprawling city, and the small circle of musicians who knew me as Atlanta Bill. As the skyscrapers of Houston faded in my rear-view mirror, I had no idea of the magnitude of what I was leaving behind. No one would ever call me Atlanta Bill again. I'd never play another harmonica solo to enthusiastic applause in the Ice House. But how furiously I would struggle for years to recapture the soul-filling elation of those Ice House nights.

CHAPTER 6

All The Crooked Roads
To Bluegrass

The most powerful motivation is rejection.
—Anonymous

This Sunday afternoon, I'm back at Lyon Park in Arlington. A guitar player kicks off a fast-paced version of "John Hardy," a bluegrass classic. He sings the verse and chorus once and then begins to pass the tune clockwise around the circle, so that each player gets a chance to play a solo over the verse of the song.

I've been to enough bluegrass jams by this time to know that, when the song leader looks straight at you, that's your signal to play. And I'm ready for this one. "John Hardy" is a tune I've played enough times with recordings to know by heart. So I wait in the happy anticipation of pleasantly surprising everyone that a bluegrass standard can be played note-for-note and up to speed on a harmonica.

The warm embrace of audiences at the Ice House

seems so very far away. Now I'm in bluegrass country, hell bent on finding a place in this unfamiliar music. This Sunday, I've brought along my Turkish toffee box of harmonicas as I ease into the circle of pickers.

But when the solo comes around to me, the leader doesn't even deign to acknowledge my presence but moves seamlessly to the next picker. His unspoken message: *If you're not playing a real bluegrass instrument, you're not wanted here.*

Hot shame flushes my face at being passed over in front of everyone. *Hey guys,* I want to blurt out, *I just want to make music with you! I know this tune by heart, and I know how to make this little mouth harp sing. Just give me a chance!* But that plea, I knew, would only make me look weak and pathetic. I've been ostracized by common, unspoken consent of the pickers, and that's just that.

In every field of human endeavor, there is a class of persons who are deemed unworthy to participate in that endeavor. In sports, it is the 97-pound weakling. In bluegrass music, it is the harmonica player. How can that musical runt ever hope to play on the varsity team?

Americans in general view the harmonica as, at best, a musical toy, at worst, an annoying noisemaker. In bluegrass, the problem is deeper than that. It's partly tradition: Bill Monroe designated the five "bluegrass instruments" as the configuration of the bluegrass ensemble: the guitar, bass, banjo, fiddle, and mandolin. Any instruments not on that list are threats to the integrity of the tradition, and most bluegrass musicians stand ready to defend that integrity at any cost.

Stories abound of harmonica players being shunned at bluegrass events. George Thacker, a fine harmonica player from Tennessee who has a couple of albums to his credit, was once scheduled to perform at a bluegrass festival with a pickup band of bluegrass musicians he'd never met. Unbeknownst to Thacker, the string players hatched a plan to undermine his performance. They synchronized their instruments a microtone down so that they all sounded sweetly coordinated. When Thacker played over their backing, however, his harmonica sounded horribly out of tune with the band. As the pickup band left the stage, the guitar player whispered to Thacker, "Too bad the harmonica's not a bluegrass instrument."

But with all the roadblocks before me, why in the world would I persist in playing an unwanted instrument in this restrictive musical genre? Why not take up a valued instrument and put all my energy into that? The answer is probably rooted in my contrarian nature, my stubborn tendency to forge ahead with my own quixotic journey and all the pitfalls it entails. Besides, there's only a tiny handful of competent bluegrass harmonica players in the entire world. Wouldn't it be wonderful to be one of those hardy few to find a place in this challenging music?

Then I discover the repertoire of old-time fiddle tunes. The old barn-dance numbers of frontier America, fiddle tunes move at a fast clip, and the melodies move around in unexpected ways. Not surprisingly, fiddle tunes are devilishly hard to play on a harmonica. The fluidity and speed a fiddler can command with her bow and the dancing fingers of her left hand are hard to even approach on the harmonica with its staccato in-and-out breathing pattern. But I still have a hunch that playing fiddle tunes note-for-note is a key, possibly *the* key, to getting respect for the harmonica in the bluegrass world.

The first hurdle is finding role models who show that this is even possible. Then, on some obscure listserv, I learn of Irvin Royal. He lives in Owensboro, Kentucky, and, like most harmonica players, he has always played his music in relative obscurity. Still, he has worked hard to get his music out to the world by making cheap cassettes of his music, which he sells by mail. His playing is a revelation to me: fast, melodic tunes played note-for-note in the old "straight harp" style, backed up with simple chordal "vamping" articulated by slapping his tongue on and off the low register of the harmonica. When I order a couple of Irvin's cassettes, I include a note to ask how he started playing. He responds with a two-page heartfelt letter, handwritten in bold block letters.

Irvin learned to play back on the family farm, listening to his father play the harmonica that he always carried in the vest pocket of his bib overalls. As Irvin progressed in his playing, he encountered a new influence in Benny Goodman's swing-era clarinet lines. He found that he could imitate some of the feel of Goodman's high-end clarinet by soulfully bending the blow notes on the upper register of his harmonica.

Still, he remained a lonely harmonica player isolated in a small town on the Ohio River. He finally found an outlet by attending fiddle festivals throughout the South. Many of these festivals used to include harmonica competitions, and Irvin won several first places in states such as Tennessee, Alabama, and North Carolina. "It's wake up time!" he wrote of these championships, which revealed that he had an unusual talent that helped spring him out of complete obscurity.

Irvin has passed away as I write this, but I can still hear his clear, bell-like single notes and his fluid, precisely articulated melody lines. So this lonely harmonica player from a town on the Ohio River became one of those teachers I've never met. His sound still echoes for me across the miles and across the years. From him, I went on to discover other isolated harmonica players—David Rice in Ohio, Mark Graham in Washington state, and Tony Eyers in Australia—who specialize in American fiddle tunes. The fast, agile playing confirmed my hunch that if I could just add fiddle tunes to my repertoire—"Whiskey Before Breakfast," "Liberty," Cherokee Shuffle," "Red Haired Boy"—I just might carve out a niche for the harmonica in Lyon Park and beyond.

Lyon Park is also the place where my first mandolin came into my hands.

Chalk it up to a generous-hearted bluegrasser. Paul Maupin grew up in east Tennessee and played guitar in college with a harmonica player, Kirk "Jelly Roll" Johnson, who went on to work in the music industry in Nashville. So, Paul had a more broad minded approach to "non-bluegrass instruments" than most pickers, and our conversation ranged far and wide. I shared my lifelong yearning to sing, and, perhaps, to accompany myself on an instrument.

The next Sunday Paul showed up with a mandolin. "I just had this one gathering dust," he said. "Why don't you take it home and try it for a while?"

"You mean you're *lending* me this?" I'd never even touched a mandolin before. I turned the shrimpy-looking instrument over in my hands. Just four pairs of strings on a short fretboard. It was a cheaply built A model, but perfectly tunable and playable.

"Sure. Keep it as long as you want."

As if this generosity weren't enough, Paul then proceeded to show me the approved bluegrass shape for making mandolin chords, which requires a claw-like stretch of the left hand across the fingerboard.

"You're kidding, right?"

He wasn't. Getting comfortable with the stretch was going to take some doing, but if I could master it, I could move the claw shape up and down the fretboard and make all the most common major chords. But I'd just turned fifty! Could these middle-aged fingers learn to adroitly move that chord shape up and down the neck, while executing the minute, rapid-fire picking motions of the right hand? Had anybody ever learned to play a stringed instrument (so anyone would want to hear it, anyway) in middle age or beyond?

Well, yes, someone had. There's the Mississippi bluesman, "T Model" Ford, for example, who didn't take up guitar until he was almost sixty. Yet he learned to finger pick well enough to have a modest success touring and recording professionally.

John Lewis Carter Ford was born around 1923 (he wasn't sure the exact year) and lived his entire life in the Mississippi Delta. He had a colorful life—he once served time on a chain gang for stabbing a man to death—so he had a lot to sing the blues about. He was married several times and claimed to have fathered 26 children ("boys and girls both," he proudly stated). When his fifth wife left him, she gave him a guitar as a farewell present, and that's how it all started.

He could never explain how he learned to play. He apparently just tried to pick out sounds that resembled the licks of guitarists he admired. Nor did he ever figure out how to tune a guitar in any of the standard ways, but the tuning he arrived at lent a haunting quality to the raw blues he played. Someone said he played "in the key of T." Along the way, he discovered that when he felt down in the dumps—he called it "a little touch of the blues"--playing the guitar took it away.

T Model started singing and playing in juke joints in Mississippi until he was discovered by a record producer. He ultimately recorded several albums and performed in blues festivals around the country, even after a stroke limited his right-hand mobility in his eighties.

So yes, T Model proved that it is possible to learn to play a stringed instrument in midlife and beyond, and maybe even tour the country with it. I don't aspire to that kind of eminence. But can I just learn to play well enough to make a decent showing at Lyon Park? The answer to that will be slow in coming and will take a long time in the woodshed.

Ironically, it was the mandolin that brought me back to the blues, in a former barbershop that sat in a row of storefronts in northeast Washington. Inside the deep and narrow interior, the musicians sat against either wall facing one another. One barber's chair remained, upholstered in green leather, a sacred relic where no one was allowed to sit. The barber was the late African American guitar legend Archie Edwards, who sponsored a blues jam every Saturday at his shop. After his death in 1998, Edwards' guitar protégé, the very tall, very dark, and very gracious Mike Baytop, started a foundation to perpetuate Archie's legacy of the Piedmont style of finger-picked guitar blues as traditionally played in Virginia and the Carolinas. I met Mike after hearing him sing at the Folklife Festival on the National Mall and he warmly invited me to "join the family" at the Archie Edward Blues Heritage Foundation every Saturday afternoon.

So here I was, back where I started, in the blues. I could have played harmonica here—the tin sandwich is fully accepted in the genre—but there was always a glut of guys with harmonicas. Anyway, I was mostly here to undertake my project of teaching myself the mandolin.

But why here, at a blues jam? The mandolin isn't normally thought of as a blues instrument—it can't cry or sing like a guitar. Was it just my crazy predilection to bring the wrong instrument to whatever musical genre I happen to be in? Except that the mandolin can be a blues instrument, at least in the hands of a few old African American blues masters such as Yank Rachell and Vol Stevens. Theirs is a small tradition stretching back to the black string bands of the twenties and thirties, and some pickers realized that the mandolin has some specific advantages in the acoustic blues. Its loud volume can project over the guitars, and it really lends itself to picking out intricate blues lines.

Not that it was going to be easy. First of all, learning to fret the mandolin *hurts*. Those skinny strings bit into the tips of the fingers of my left hand, and I was born with sensitive skin. The good news for prospective mandolin players is that, if you stick with it for about three weeks, you build up calluses and the pain will go away.

I was still having trouble with the requirement that, in playing rhythmic backup, the mandolin is supposed to stress the offbeats of a song. It seemed I couldn't get away from the habit of stressing the downbeats. That won't work in the blues—or in bluegrass either, because Bill Monroe borrowed that offbeat groove from the African American tradition. There was no quick fix for my paleface rhythm, but through dogged online research I discovered a cluster of practice routines that would begin to uncover the mystery of rhythm to this rhythmically challenged player.

At the barber shop, I stumbled along with my usual roundabout way of self-teaching —just sitting at the periphery of the group of musicians, trying to accompany them by slow trial and error. I'd pluck one note of the song in time with the music: plunk-plunk-plunk. Then perhaps a second note in time—plunkplunk-plunk-plunk—just trying to find part of the tune with those two notes. Above all, I opened my ears to the tune, trying to hear where the chords changed, listening intently to what the guitars were doing. It was a slow but not uninteresting process, because I was actually taking part in the music. I'd see other beginning musicians come to the shop and, out of fear, never play the first note. But I just had faith that over a period of months, my picking hand would eventually graduate to plunkety-plunkety-plunk-plunk and finally to something resembling the tune being played. One day, though, the miracle happened. I played an acceptable blues solo, high up and trembling, when my turn came around.

When one of our family reunions takes place in DC, I invite Chris to the barbershop jam. He's brought the pawnshop Fender up from Florida, where he moved to work on the space shuttle for a subcontractor for NASA. As a guitarist, Chris is still the solitary adept who'd learned to play on lonely afternoons on the barrier island, but I had a hunch he'd enjoy the chance to take turns playing leads in an organized blues jam. When we take our places in the circle and Chris's turn comes around, I feel a surge of pride to see my strong son, tanned by the Florida sun, turning heads in the barbershop with his his confident picking. Chris comes back from the shop glowing, proud that he held his own with those seasoned guitar pickers.

So has this been a bonding moment that could bring father and son, with our diverging musical journeys, closer at last?

Well, not quite. A one-off jam session won't be enough to close the gap between father and son. On a subsequent family reunion at Chris's Florida home near the beach, I come prepared with my mandolin. But the first afternoon of our visit, while watching my grandkids, William and Anna, splashing in Chris's backyard pool, I happen to look though the sliding glass door—and there is Chris, playing guitar, completely on his own except for an electronic backing track. He looks totally focused, unaware of anyone else in the world, including his father.

I think it is wonderful that a self-taught musician is still passionate about a hobby he learned in his teens. Still, I am crestfallen that he didn't suggest that we play a duet. And yes, I could have taken the initiative and proposed just that. But if it hasn't even occurred to Chris, what's the point? So I just shrug and go back to watching my grandkids splashing in the pool.

CHAPTER 7

Stumbling Into Song

Little drum, little drum,
Help me sing.
So that my voice comes out
So that my voice comes out
And gets where it has to go.
      —Abuelita Malinalli

This Sunday afternoon, the gospel singers are sitting in a rough circle in Kathie's living room on a quiet, tree-lined street in Takoma Park, not far from the VFW post where I take my chances at bluegrass every other Monday night. This Sunday afternoon, I've come to the monthly gospel sing sponsored by the local folklore society, and I'm here to find out if I can sing.

I've always been pretty sure I can't. This is strange because I grew up in a singing household. My Dad had a beautiful tenor voice and had made extra money in college traveling around to local churches as part of a hymn-singing quartet. Oddly enough, though, his sweet, tuneful singing around the house, rather than encouraging me to try my voice at it, had the opposite effect. *If that's what singing is,* was my unconscious reaction, *I'll never be able to do it.* The very notion of trying to sing with or in front of others seemed an invitation to public shaming. Later I learn that there is even a term—decantaphobia—for that fear.

Still, I've always yearned to raise my voice in song. So once again, I'm taking that risk at the gospel sing that meets once a month, each time in a different singer's home. It isn't a worship service—unbelievers like me are welcome. It's about the love of singing, specifically singing the old-time, foot-stomping Southern gospel numbers—"Beulah Land," "Turn Your Radio On," "I'll Fly Away," and, of course, "Amazing Grace."

Once again, I'm on pins and needles in an unknown situation. The soundtrack playing in my head is all too familiar. I don't belong here. I can't sing on key. Better not sing out loud—just mouth the words. But when Kathie, today's ebullient hostess, hands me a couple of songbooks, her welcoming smile goes a long way toward calming my nerves.

"Let's do a blood song!" someone calls out, and another singer offers "Washed in the Blood," one of a subgenre of songs that draw on the gory imagery of the Crucifixion. With a radiant smile that belies the grim lyrics, Kathie herself kicks off the song with infectious energy:

Have you been to Jesus for the cleansing power?
Are you washed in the blood of the lamb?

It's a real foot stomper. The singers, some closer to pitch than others, raise a joyful noise that fills the living room. Uncertain about my own pitch, I begin to sing along, very tentatively at first, then a bit louder. Ever alert to signs that things are going badly, I cast my eyes around the room for fishy-eyed looks in my direction. Seeing none, I begin to relax a little. And sing a bit less tentatively.

When we break for a potluck dinner, I sidle up to Kathie and ask almost under my breath, "Tell me gently—am I singing in tune?"

"Sounds good to me!" Kathie's answer isn't resoundingly reassuring, but it leaves the possibilities open.

I return the next month and sing a bit louder. The next month, a bit louder still. It will take many sessions with the gospel group to begin to trust my ears that I am really singing in tune (well, mostly), but I finally relax and come into a kind of singing confidence. I begin singing loudly and lustily, giving vent to that pent-up energy and emotion from inside me that music allows to come out and be heard.

Eventually I'm belting out lyrics without fear, filling my lungs with air and letting it pulse across my vocal chords. Thank heaven for the safe haven of the gospel group, where anyone can make mistakes without penalty. I wish every gun-shy singer could find such an outlet.

But if the gospel group is a safe, sunny backwater for a beginner overcoming his self-doubt, rip tides and high winds await in the bluegrass culture. There will be a few near-death experiences like the one at Lyon Park when my singing is so bad that two of the players immediately walk away, and I feel as though I'm falling through the floor (or wanting to) with humiliation. A bluegrass Samaritan comes to the rescue: Lynn, an excellent singer and guitarist who coaxes me through the rest of the song. Without her kindness, my only option would have been to quietly slink away, never to return to the place where aspirations to sing come to die.

But return I do to run the fatal risk again and again, driven by some blind desire to find my voice. I do some of the right things. I sit down and memorize the lyrics to a number of standards, so that I'll never (or rarely) stumble over the words again. I practice the songs with my mandolin, trying to coordinate the timing of the chunk-chunk-chunk with my singing.

But I fail to do one thing that would help the most: take singing lessons. Too pricey, I tell my frugal self. So I just keep showing up at the VFW and Lyon Park, learning in the most aimless, inefficient way: by trial and error. If something I sing is spurned, I try not to do that again—that is, if I can figure out what it I did that was wrong. If it's accepted, I take a deep breath and move forward. It's a rambling, roundabout way to learn. Lessons would have been so worth it.

Somewhere along the way, though, I do find my voice—a not unpleasant, twangy baritone. It certainly has its shortcomings, such as drifting off pitch without warning. It can't handle songs with big interval jumps, but it can generally carry a simple down-home tune. I'm gradually learning how to relax, even under pressure, and let the breath come out from somewhere just above my gut. I'm surprised to discover that my singing voice is loud and penetrating—something that, as a quiet introvert, I would never have guessed. And gradually, I am beginning to lose my fear of leading others in song.

Finally comes the day where the miracle seems to happen. An old-time jam is just wrapping up at the annual midwinter folk festival in Takoma Park, and the monitor asks if someone wants to lead a song.

Yes, let me step off that cliff. I volunteer. But what might we sing?

"Do you know 'I'll Fly Away'?" asks the monitor.

Sure I know it—I've sung it dozens of times at the gospel sing. The monitor nods me the go ahead; not giving myself time to lose my nerve, I take a deep breath and kick off the first verse:

One bright morning when this life is o'er, I'll fly away....

Chopping what I hope is a steady backbeat on the mandolin, I make it through the first verse with the guitars providing me a full bed of music. When I come to the chorus, everyone who understands the mysteries of singing harmony (and some who don't) joins in, and the sound swells to fill the room. Some singers have their eyes closed, a sign that this simple music is touching something inside them. Then I call out "fiddles!" and the fiddlers wail for sixteen bars—a huge sound that fills the room even more.

On the next verse, as I pull the lyrics from deep in my lungs, a swelling euphoria—the feeling I used to get blowing the harmonica at the Ice House—rises up inside me. But I'm not the star of this Opry—if anything, I'm the caller at a country square dance. Then we belt out the final chorus—*I'll fly away, O glory*—with all the expression our vocal cords can muster, and it's over. The joy in the room is almost palpable.

"Good job!" says the monitor, and I leave the room feeling as if I'm walking on air. And yes, I'm sensing that there's a place at the end of some musical rainbow where the "we" is more soul-filling than the *"me"*.

Back at the Takoma Park gospel group, I'm getting even more surprises about the ways singing can open doors in one's heart that you didn't know were there. I came to this group with the utilitarian goal of finding out if I could sing. Now I find myself falling in love with these primitive old songs, many of which my forebears in the Blue Ridge Mountains would have found so familiar—and so comforting. Unlike them, I've never been a believer. Strangely enough though, I now find that the joy of singing provides an entrée into the world of faith my ancestors would have understood, a world overseen by a loving and forgiving Creator. And how uplifting that does feel; even if only for the space of the gospel song, to feel the release that my forbearers must have felt in belting out these great old lyrics.

> *O how sweet to walk in this pilgrim way,/Leaning on the everlasting arms/O how bright the path grows from day to day/Leaning on the everlasting arms.*

I'm not about to become a convert to primitive Christianity—for better or for worse, I'm just too much a product of skeptical modernity. But I treasure my sojourns, however short they may be, to that place of unquestioned Love and Light. One Sunday afternoon in Takoma Park I feel particularly transported. We're at the home of Barbara, a devoted gardener who has transformed her back yard into a space that looks and feels like a Garden of Eden. As it happens, my brother Bolling, who is a devout Christian, seems to be on his deathbed, back in his home in a hill town in the Georgia mountains. Sitting in this marvelous garden, lifting my voice to the heavens with Barbara, Kathie, and the others, I feel as though I'm singing Bolling home.

Turns out I'm mistaken: Bolling takes a turn for the better and is still very much in his body. But that doesn't invalidate my joy of entering the sacred space of song and singing someone into the Light—something I never dreamed I'd experience. Singing, it seems, might have more to offer than just pretty notes.

Sketching The Sketchers

*Perhaps the artist's only gift is a peculiar quality
of attention. While she minds the trivial details
of balance and form, the soul can slip free, have
a clear run toward its truth, the truth for which it
came into this world.*
  —Mary Rose O'Reilly,
    The Love of Impermanent Things

We all gather in a semicircle around the facilitator, a young woman museum staffer who holds a degree in art history. Every Tuesday afternoon the Smithsonian American Art Museum hosts the "Draw and Discover" program. It is held is a space overlooking the top floor of the museum, where a sturdy catwalk with railings calls to mind something out of a vintage ocean liner. This is the Luce Center where, recessed into nooks off the catwalk, is a treasure trove of paintings by American artists like William H. Johnson, Ben Shahn, and Philip Evergood. "Draw and Discover" encourages anyone interested in trying their hand at sketching to wander through the nooks and copy an artwork of their choosing, usually in colored pencil on toned paper provided by the museum.

The young museum staffer delivers a brief talk on some aspect of art history from which she derives a drawing "challenge" to give the sketchers something to work toward. When she stops talking, I stand up.

"I'm not doing the challenge today," I say. "I'd like to do something different—draw a portrait of one of you as you draw. I call it 'Sketching the Sketchers.' I hope that's okay."

After Jackie Saunders' portraiture class, I'm trying to take my portraits to the next level. My classes with Avis and Jackie are all well and good, but I cut my teeth drawing out on the street, and that is still my preferred venue. I still love the challenge of taking my "models" where I find them, not necessarily hired and posed.

Some of the attendees at the Luce Center, though, look dubious at the prospect of being sketched by a stranger. I am starting to realize that women can be skittish about being sketched, particularly if the portrait is rigorously true to life (i.e., sans flattery). And, as the participants scatter into the nooks around the catwalk, I'm tasked with finding a sketcher who will allow me to sketch him or her in the narrow confines of a nook. Some understand that I'm offering, in the spirit of art, to create a good likeness of them. Others, perhaps feeling that I'm invading their personal space, flatly refuse. I'm not one to let rejection run off my back, so the refusal stings.

Today, though, I am lucky—I come upon Rick, a bald, soft-spoken man about my own age wearing a multicolored vest. Rick doesn't copy the artworks in the Luce Center but instead pens colorful hieroglyphs in colored ink on small drawing pad. He's perfectly comfortable with my sketching him, and I settle on a stool to sketch. I pull out my old-fashioned fountain pen and, starting with a key feature—in Rick's case, the eyes—I focus on them as if the nib of my pen were actually touching the edges of his features, just the way Nicolaïdes' book taught me. I only look at the paper to make sure my pen lines are not going completely astray.

Mary Rose O'Reilly, a contemporary Minnesota poet writes that attention is key to the artist's journey. And today at the Luce Center, my quality of attention is intense. The future and past don't exist—I am right here, now, in this shining moment with the impromptu "model" in front of me. All that matters is coaxing the ink lines to coalesce into the hoped-for likeness and to catch the concentration Rick is putting into his own drawing. Next, I take out a brush pen filled with diluted ink and lay in the shadows and the dark areas of clothing—and so quickly the sketch is done. The best part is its "in the moment" quality. There is no self-conscious artiste present, just a state of flow in which all attention is focused on capturing the figure in my field of vision.

When we sketchers gather back for a show-and-tell session, however, my critical faculties come to the fore. As one sketcher after another holds up his or her artless copy of a famous painting for praise and comment, I wonder: Why on earth am I sitting through this parade of half-baked drawings? But the sketchers are uniformly supportive of one another, praising the efforts of their peers, whether deserving or not.

But when I hold up my drawing of Rick in front the group, the oohs and aahs are noticeably louder, and (I tell myself) more sincere. And that sincerity is sweet honey to my ears.

Have I so quickly forgotten that, while I was sketching Rick, the state of my ego was of no concern? I was in the "flow" of interpreting a clothed human form. When Mary Rose O'Reilly wrote about the artist's soul slipping free, I don't think she was talking about this yearning after accolades.

O my fickle soul, how little resolute you are, when the least change of circumstance can blow you off course!

It's Monday, and I'm back at the Torpedo Factory, but not for a class this time. This is Open Life Studio, offering a professional, posed model and no instruction of any kind. None, that is, except what I can glean from watching Jackie Saunders, who comes to the studio, not to teach, but just to create her own wonderful drawings and watercolors.

Open Life goes from 10 a.m. to 3 p.m., with a short break for lunch—a generous swath of time for those who are serious about their art. And indeed, the artists at their easels are a more serious lot than I've seen so far. Some have degrees in painting and are skilled at watercolor or acrylics. Above all, there's Jackie. She doesn't mind if I look over her shoulder as her magical figure studies and portraits flow out of her dip pen and her watercolor brush. The freedom to observe a master at work is both instructive and inspiring, and I go back to my easel and churn out sketch after sketch.

Whenever the model takes a break, the artists can wander around the studio, examining what each has done. Some may pause to admire a certain artist's work, and I hear exclamations of admiration. They rarely exclaim at my easel, and if they do stop, it's only time for a seemingly dismissive glance. After this occurs for several sessions, the fragile egg of my need for approval begins to crack.

One woman who consistently garners praise paints figures in acrylic that, to my eye, are distorted and bulbous and painted in hues that bear no relation to the planes and curves of the body. Granted, that's a matter of taste, and one afternoon DeAnn, a studio regular, looks at the woman's latest concoction and purrs, "Bravo! Just marvelous. No further refinement needed."

Then, turning to me, she brightly announces, "And

Bill's just cranking 'em out."

I flush with hot indignation. She may have meant this as a compliment for my high productivity, but I take it as a grievous slight.

"So it's quantity over quality?" I blurt out. "That's not good." Henceforth DeAnn will give my easel a very wide berth.

At the end of the day, I leave the Torpedo Factory in a snit that stays with me the entire fifteen-minute walk to the Braddock Road Metro stop. I'm beginning to realize that my hunger for accolades, and snits when I don't get them, are a serious roadblock to a happy journey into art.

The library at the Quaker Meeting is totally silent this Monday morning. This is when our Buddhist sangha community meets, and Hugh Byrne, our teacher, is already seated in a comfortable armchair in the corner, his eyes closed. Hugh is on the faculty of the Insight Meditation Center of Washington, and he spends every Monday morning with us to open our minds to the tradition of Vipassana meditation, a way of self-transformation through simply observing our thoughts and feelings as they emerge. As the Christian faith loses traction in unprogrammed Meetings like ours, many Friends are increasingly looking to Buddhism as a spiritual path. That's why Hugh is here every Monday morning.

A Londoner of Irish descent and probably the wisest person I have ever met, Hugh always reminds us to pay attention to the present moment, with the goal of remaining conscious and aware as we go through our day. Of course, most of us think we are already fully aware, but in reality our minds are generally clouded with nonstop ruminations on the past and future. To be fully alive to the present, as the Vipassana tradition teaches, sounds awfully simple, but we all find that applying that teaching to daily life can be a slippery goal.

We begin our Monday morning gatherings with a half hour of silent meditation, and a few regulars are already here, eyes closed, sitting in deep silence. But the door of the library remains open, and the latecomers will continue to straggle in throughout the meditation period, distracting my efforts to center down into a quiet place within myself. So I slip away into a darkened alcove off the reading room. Closing the sliding door behind me, I select a straight-backed chair and feel the weight of my body as I hold the intention to center down into quietude.

When I first started meditating, that inner quiet remained elusive. My mind would race off into a nonstop stream of endless subvocal chatter, one thought begetting another without my being able to stop them. Lately, though, the thought stream seems to be slowing down and growing quieter as I follow the fluted rhythm of my breath. I'm finding that I can let go of making to-do lists, planning the menu for dinner, and ruminating about a perceived slight from someone last week. And today, the thoughts slacken and ease to the point where, if only for a moment, there's just a sense of consciousness that is quietly, impersonally aware of itself. It's a place all its own: a dark, still pool behind my eyes where thought comes to an end. There's nothing ecstatic about it—in fact, it has no emotional taste at all, but it seems important to know that the dark, still pool exists and that thoughts can find their place in silence there, if only for a moment.

Hugh has said that I shouldn't retreat into the darkened alcove to meditate. He thinks I should sit with the others, even the stragglers, *because* they irritate me, and because getting to the root of such irritation and aversion is one key to self-understanding. *Follow the suffer-*

ing, he often says, the feelings that things are not as they should be, because if we can track back to what we're clinging to, we can begin to understand in what way we are not seeing things as they really are.

I respect Hugh's wisdom enough to have no doubt he's right, but I'm still not ready to try to let go of my irritation with the latecomers straggling into the room. Anyway, when I sit in that little side room, I've been able to see the still dark pool and the end of thoughts. How many in the sangha can say that?

Admittedly, the inner peace I find in the darkened side room doesn't carry over into the rest of my day. It certainly doesn't go with me with my next session of life drawing. There's a disconnect. Fortunately, I can talk about that in the sangha. I lay it all out: my craving for praise and my snits when I don't get it. And today, the response of the group has a bit of tough love in it.

"You shouldn't be focused on praise," declares Marcia, a longtime participant in the sangha. "Making art should be its own reward."

Boy, does that sound pompous, I say to myself. *Have you ever drawn the human figure, and do you know how hard it is to do it well? Anyway, doesn't every artist crave fame, or affirmation at the very least?*

Linda, another regular in the Buddhist sit, turns to me. "Do you really enjoy those drawing sessions?"

Linda's question catches me up short. How strange that I have never actively considered that question. "Yes!" I say emphatically, and to myself, *Of course I enjoy it!*

But do I really? It's becoming increasingly clear I've been focusing on the end product—actually, other artists' reaction to it rather than on the drawing experience itself. "Your yearning for praise is really getting in the way of your experience of drawing, of art," says Hugh.

Okay, Hugh, I already knew that. But what Hugh says next is jolting: He offers a daunting prescription for my conundrum.

"In your next studio," he says, "practice watching your reactions as they arise. Don't judge them or try to change them, just watch. Make your practice your main goal in the studio. Make the art secondary."

Make the art secondary? But isn't making art the whole point of spending a whole day in the studio? But Hugh insists that, when we simply pay attention to difficult states without judging them, they lose their afflictive energy. They dissipate.

Sounds too good to be true, says the skeptic in me. But I'm unhappy enough to give it a try. On my next visit to the Torpedo Factory, I'll see what dissipates and what doesn't.

I don't have to wait long to try it out. At the first break, I stand at my easel where my latest good drawing rests ignored as I listen to cooing praise for others' productions. And I feel the resentment rising up in me, bilious.

Buddhism teaches that there is a faculty of the mind known as "the one who watches"—the capacity to look with detachment at the contents of the mind, such as thoughts that flow through it, somewhat like watching a silent film. Previously, when resentment arose, it would overtop my consciousness. There'd be no room for anything except that flood of hurt and anger. Today, though, I sense an opening, a twilit awareness that seems capable of holding thoughts and feelings like stones in a dark vase. I take a deep breath and center down into that awareness.

And there it is. I can almost visualize it: solid, dark, and sour, my resentment—an afflictive object that I can dimly perceive as if under smoked glass. I wait for it to dissipate, the way Hugh said it would. It doesn't. It hangs there, immutable and toxic in my mind's eye.

But then I realize something: If I can view my resentment as if it were a foreign object, it's not the whole of me. It may be toxic, but it doesn't have the power to engulf my consciousness. With that realization, its energy begins to slacken, to lose some of its toxicity. It may not be today, but maybe I'll see the day soon when resentment won't cause me to walk to the subway in a snit.

Hugh is right: The art studio is a perfect laboratory for watching one's inner states, including the arising of clinging and aversion. After all, there is really nothing at stake here--nobody is going to lambaste my drawings in front of everybody. My hurt feelings, my suffering, are manufactured almost entirely by me. And, as the Buddha promised in the Four Noble Truths, there is a path to the end of suffering.

Funny how this art journey can be about so much more than just making pictures.

*A year and a half after leaving the magazine,
I am still adjusting to retired life. Music and
drawing, I find, are wonderful ways forward, but
something is missing.*

There are nights when I suffer from insomnia. When this happens, Ann offers to hug me back to sleep. Sometimes it works. Other times, Ann, her arm around me, quickly falls back to sleep herself while I lie awake, staring at the ceiling.

I am learning to deal with my new, anxiety-fueled sleeping patterns. One discovery is that I can enjoy great literature in sleepless hours by downloading audiobooks to a mobile listening device. My favorite audiobooks are in Spanish, which I learned in my youth. Listening to them, I can keep up and even improve my listening skills in that beautiful language while being lulled back to sleep. So maybe insomnia can have a kind of silver lining. In months of nightly listening, I slowly absorb entire novels, including Garcia Marquez's lengthy masterpiece, *Cien Años de Soledad.*

Other nights, I have bad dreams. I dream about being back at the magazine, but I'm not back at my corner office, overseeing an editorial staff. Instead, I'm a lowly intern, toiling away without pay at a borrowed desk. I'm skulking around in the shadows, fearful that Patricia will see me and throw me out. These are dreams of humiliation and loss of place, status, and dignity, and they tell me that the grief over the loss of my beloved job still haunts me.

The dreams also tell me that I yearn to write again. I yearn to touch other minds through the intimate telepathy of the written word, which was my first love. I yearn to shape sentences and paragraphs that, when I read them back to myself, almost sing on the page. I yearn to do again what I probably do the best of anything. And I know that, even in my late sixties, I still have a lot of writing left in me.

So to write again, but what? Writing more magazine articles doesn't inspire. I need to find an all-consuming project that will call forth all my mental and psychological resources–probably a book-length project that will require extensive research. But really, long or short is not the point; I want to write something beautiful. And powerful. And moving. I want to dance again in the fires of creation.

First, though, I need something absolutely moving to write about.

That's how I got to Shanksville.

CHAPTER 9

A Long Road Back to a Hard Way Forward

Sé que aún me queda una oportunidad
Sé que aún no es tarde para recapacitar . . .
Con los años que me quedan por vivir . . .
["I know I have I still have a chance. I know
it's not too late to start anew, in the years I
have left to live . . . "]
　　　　—Gloria Estefan

In the beginning, there was nothing here but a bleak
hillside, the scar tissue of a former strip mine. Then, on
September 11, 2001, United Flight 93 exploded into the
bottom of the hill at 500 miles an hour, sending a pil-
lar of fire and smoke hundreds of feet into the air. Nothing was left but an enormous crater and the vaporized
remains of forty passengers and crew.

The people of Somerset County, Pennsylvania, and
especially the village of Shanksville, only two miles from
the crash site, were traumatized by the disaster that had

fallen on their doorstep. But they were also inspired, even reverent, because before they died, the passengers and crew on that airplane rose up as one and revolted against the terrorists. So the airliner ended its last flight, not in Washington, DC as the terrorists apparently planned, but here, at the bottom of this scarred hillside. Because the passengers fought back, Flight 93 became the only hijacked plane that did not reach its destination---and thus became an inspiration to a traumatized nation.

In the weeks following the crash, the good people of Shanksville came out to this bleak hillside and, on their own initiative, erected a memorial to those heroic dead. It was not a thing of beauty—just a tall, unadorned chain-link fence, but it quickly became a people's memorial—a place for Americans to hang tributes in homage to the forty dead. And come they did, from all over the country—first a trickle, then in their hundreds, then in their thousands, every month. Soon the entire fence was filled with heartfelt messages scrawled on everything from paper plates to caps to teddy bears. The visitors felt a powerful impulse to leave something to honor the forty Americans who stood up and fought to their last breath. Their most common message was Never Forget.

A few years after the crash, I made my own pilgrimage to the chain-link memorial for a very personal reason. I was in my office at the magazine on 9/11, just blocks away from the White House and the Capitol, the likely targets of the hijacked plane. If all had worked out as the terrorists planned, I would, at the very least, have borne witness to the fire and mayhem that was visited on lower Manhattan. I was spared that because of the bravery of the passengers and crew. So this detour to view their final resting place of their remains was mostly to pay my respects.

In those first years after the crash, the place wasn't easy to find. I had driven up on the historic Lincoln Highway but didn't see a sign of any kind. So I meandered down bumpy two-lane roads until I rounded a corner and saw an angel, or rather, a tall steel sculpture of an angel, mutely pointing the way.

Honestly, though, the crash site and memorial were something of a letdown. There was nothing to see. The 757 had hit the ground with such terrible force that it literally buried itself in the earth; anything that remained above ground was fragmentary, including any body parts that had not been incinerated in the crash. Moreover, the impact crater and any other vestige of the crash had long since been backfilled, so there was nothing to see, nothing to mark the cataclysm that had been visited on this Pennsylvania hillside.

Photo Courtesy National Park Service

There was a crowd of people milling around the fence, gazing reverently at the tributes. I stood apart from them, wishing I could be alone to absorb this place on my own terms. It would have helped if there were a trail down to the place where the plane hit, where I might have walked around and pondered the meaning of it all. But that was off limits to visitors. I was restricted to the temporary memorial, hemmed in by a guard rail and abuzz with visitors.

Still, most Americans who made pilgrimages here didn't need to ponder its meaning. They knew. There had been an attack on the nation, and there could be only one proper response: solidarity with the passengers and crew who took the fight back to the terrorists. Thing of beauty or not, the chain-link fence and its load of tributes was a perfectly democratic expression of the thousands who had made pilgrimages here before me and who had come to view the crash site as sacred ground.

Then a local woman positioned herself and began to speak to the handful of people assembled here. She was Sally, one of the "ambassadors," local volunteers who greeted visitors to the site. I sat down on one of the benches to listen. Sally lived just on the other side of the trees, she said. She had felt the impact of the Boeing 757 and smelled the jet fuel when it crashed. She showed us a scrapbook of the forty passengers and crew who had taken the fight back to the terrorists. Every one of them, she said, made a difference that day. She was sure we'd all do the same.

Listening to Sally it dawned on me that the temporary memorial wasn't meant for self-styled philosophers to be alone with their thoughts. It was a blunt, unapologetic celebration of patriotism and sacrifice. All that mattered here was that, in a time of great crisis, the country pulled together. When Sally stopped talking, I had to wipe my eyes.

It's been five years since that visit, and here I am again. This weekend, on the ten-year anniversary of September 11, I will see a very different memorial. The chain-link fence will be gone, replaced by a professionally designed memorial built to last for centuries. It has taken a full decade of planning and fundraising to build it. This weekend will mark its public unveiling and dedication.

The National Park Service sponsored an international design competition that received more than a thousand entries, from which they selected "Crescent of Embrace" by Paul Murdoch, an architect from Beverly Hills, California. I've already seen presentation drawings of it. It looks very sleek, very modern—the very opposite of chain-link and makeshift. But I can't help wondering: will a sleek and serene design by a Beverly Hills architect call forth the same raw emotion as the jury-rigged "people's memorial"?

I am also different than I was at my first visit. I'm an out-of-work writer trying to find his way back to his craft. It's almost two years now since I walked out of my office in downtown DC, never to return. I think I've used the down time well, plowing more time and energy into learning to play and sing folk and country music and dive into portrait and figure drawing. But I desperately want to write again. And this topic, the ten-year struggle to build this memorial, seems tailor made for a book, and I seem well positioned to write it.

I know a lot about disaster memorials. I have been following the grim tide of mass killings in this country, and the memorials built to commemorate them, through articles we published in the magazine. Oklahoma City. Columbine. Virginia Tech. The Pentagon. I know what the design issues are and what the memorials are supposed to accomplish in the way of public memory. I have hunches about what kinds of memorial designs touch people's hearts, and which don't. So I'm well prepared to write about the Flight 93 effort. Or think I am.

There's no longer any problem finding the site. A professionally designed sign points us to our turn off the highway and onto a line of cars inching up a newly paved entry road. We end up parking illegally by the side of the road where the road crests a hill. As Ann struggles to parallel park, a man stops and tells us through the open car window. "Today is all about gratitude. Forty people gave their lives for us, for our country, and we're here to say, 'Thank you.'"

That sentiment will set me apart from most of the thousands of attendees at the two-day dedication. They bring a sense of reverence and raw patriotism inspired by the passenger revolt. My attitude is one of intense curiosity, a passion to wrap my mind around the impact of the crash of Flight 93 on this rural heartland—but for the book, always for the book. In that sense, I'm an inter-

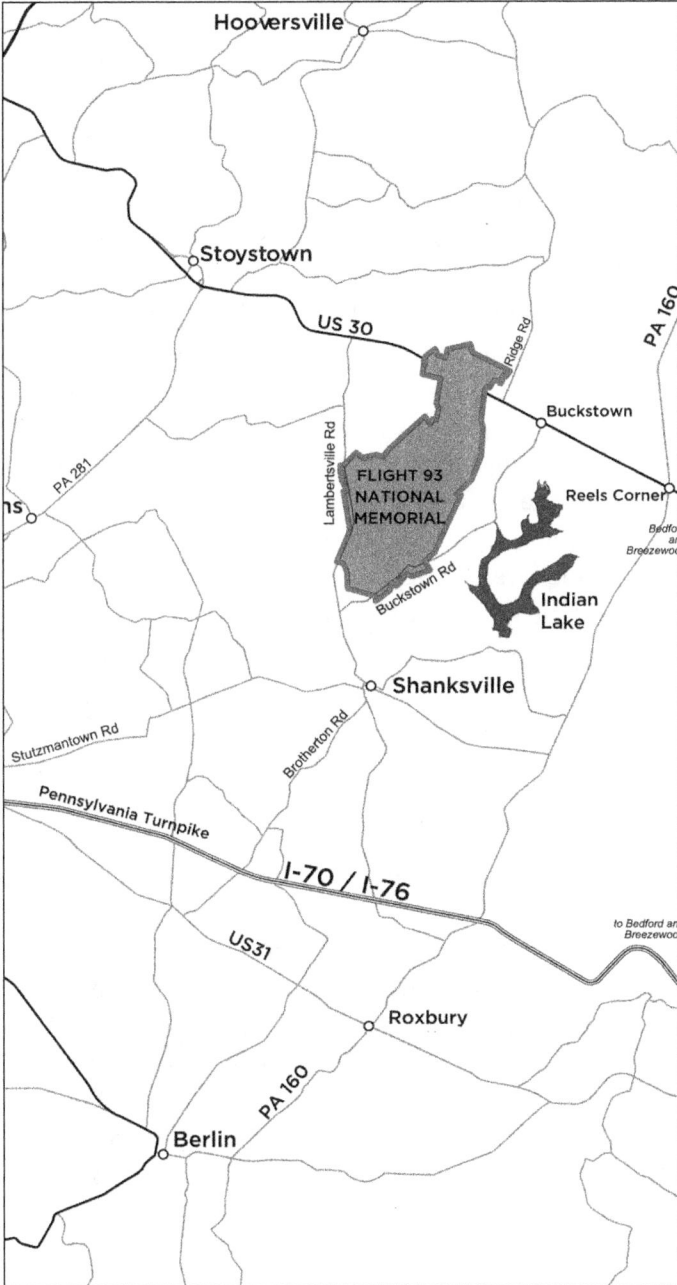

loper, almost an intruder on what most here will view as a sacred patriotic rite.

But finally, we're here, and Ann and I will finally set eyes on the Memorial Plaza. We round a curve in the road and gaze down the hill. I point to the bottom of a bowl of land where I know Flight 93 exploded into the earth and where the Memorial Plaza now rests. And there it is, a slender, unadorned line of black concrete that traces the flight path of the 757 in its final, fatal descent.

"Is that *it?*" asks Ann. And indeed, from the hill above the crash site, it is hard to imagine that that crooked line across the valley floor was worth tens of millions of dollars and ten turbulent years of planning and organization. But that is it—the Memorial Plaza, the first and most iconic component of the Flight 93 National Memorial. In a few years a fully appointed visitor's center will overlook the site, but today the black concrete line is all there is and will always be the beating heart of the Flight 93 Memorial.

It isn't until Ann and I join hundreds of other visitors walking down the 900-foot-long crooked walkway that constitutes the Memorial Plaza that we understand the intent of this stark, unrelenting line of black concrete. Nothing but a low, sloping retaining wall separates us from the "sacred ground" where the Boeing 757 exploded into the earth and where the vaporized remains of the passengers and crew will be forever interred. This is, in fact, the cemetery of the forty passengers and crew, all of them reduced to ashes by the fiery crash. Whatever remains of them must stay here always. For the past decade only family members have had access to this site, in effect the cemetery of forty people. Now, however, I can almost reach out and touch it.

As Ann and I walk down the plaza, my earlier doubts–whether a sleek and sophisticated design could ever rise to the emotional heights of the temporary "people's memorial"—fall away. The architect's design decision to have the Memorial Plaza butt up against the sacred ground is giving me what I'd wanted on my first visit to Shanksville five years earlier—the ability to walk next to the crash site and ponder the meaning of it all. This stark memorial design allows—no, forces—me to construct my own narrative of what this place means.

Photo Courtesy National Park Service

I've thought a lot about what makes an effective disaster memorial. First of all, it shouldn't sugar-coat the enormity of what happened. And this memorial doesn't. Absolutely nothing in the design, no uplifting inscriptions, no inspiring statuary softens the realization that this is the graveyard for the victims of a mass murder. Some visitors might find that cold and unforgiving, but I find it respectful of the dead and, above all, honest.

Today's dedication ceremony is a somber and well-orchestrated tribute to the passenger revolt that happened exactly ten years ago. Potent symbols abound. When an honor guard holding aloft the American and Pennsylvania flags marches between the rows of attendees seated on folding chairs, the crowd rises to its feet. With the flags positioned on the raised stage, an African American woman sings a restrained but nevertheless beautiful a capella rendition of the National Anthem. When the names of the forty dead are read aloud, local volunteers strike two enormous bells for each name, after which a bagpiper in Scots regalia pipes "Amazing Grace."

Then, one by one, the dignitaries step up to the microphone to speak, and I am reminded how political speeches so often seem so turgid and predictable. We get speeches by the US Secretary of the Interior, the Director of the National Park Service, the Governor of Pennsylvania, and the CEO of some corporation that donated a lot of money to the memorial. Then there are the former presidents, George W. Bush and Bill Clinton who, predictably, cast the passenger revolt in military terms and circle around a single theme: that the Flight 93 passengers and crew deliberately brought the airliner down on this spot, in Bush's words, to save people on the ground. This mantra, first enunciated by Bush himself when he declared the War on Terror after 9/11, has become accepted as fact by most Americans. As I dig into the research on the doomed flight, I will begin to question that accepted narrative. But that questioning is all in the future. When Bush finishes speaking, the crowd of grateful Americans leaps to their feet in an ovation. A scattered few of us, recalling Bush's military fiascos in the Middle East, remain stubbornly in our seats.

Finally, a speech that rises out of that thematic rut. Robert Pinsky, the US Poet Laureate, takes the podium to reflect on the phenomenon of memory.

"A people, any people, is what it remembers," says Pinsky, "and for the American people, Flight 93—because we remember it—has become a significant part of what we are as a people, whether we want to remember it or not." Then, surprisingly, he adds, "No one wanted to remember this event. We didn't want the burden, as well as the honor, of this memory."

Didn't want to remember it? Then what's the purpose of a memorial, anyway? But Pinsky's words are echoed and reinforced by Gordie Felt, the spokesman for the bereaved families and whose brother died in the crash, who takes the podium and talks about the duty to remember.

"Nothing frightens me more," he begins, "than the phrase 'Time heals all pain.' Do we really want to be fully healed if the end result involves the complete elimination of the pain that links us to all that we lost that morning? Let us not allow time to heal all of our pain. Let us never forget the horror of September 11. This site will forever stand as a tribute to forty individuals who, under the most horrific conditions, chose to stand as one and fight. Our painful remembrance honors them and keeps them alive in our hearts."

One final speaker commands my attention, but not for anything he says. Wally Miller, the self-described "hick coroner" who oversaw the crash site for two years and ministered directly to family members, will be the least articulate but most emotional speaker in the two-day dedication. A tall, lanky figure in a business suit, he's already daubing his eyes before donning dark glasses to hide them as he steps up to the podium.

"Pardon me if I don't look up," he says, "It will go a lot better this way." Miller's voice continues to break as he reads a selection of lines to which the audience is supposed to respond with the refrain, "We will remember them." The response is tepid, but Miller plows doggedly through his lines before sitting back down and weeping bitterly into his handkerchief.

I'm left wondering: How could a professional coroner, who routinely sees death, picks up corpses from the place they died and prepares them for burial, be so affected by the memory of the crash these ten years after it happened? Ultimately, this will provoke a broader question: How has the memory of this terrible event shaped or reshaped the lives of anyone and everyone in Shanksville?

As I frame these questions, the writer in me stirs and starts to come alive. Questions were always my M.O. as a writer—my way of identifying and grappling with the issues underlying any topic. And now the meaning of the ten-year memorial process shifts for me, and the proposed book suddenly seems to have a backbone. Now it's about the multiple faces of *memory*: memory as ennobling, connecting us, the living, to those lost loved ones and the courageous action they took that terrible morning. But also memory as pain—the pain of loss that never goes away, the heart that will always be broken. My book, if it sees the light of publication, might be a memorial in its own right to the crash.

As Ann and I depart the dedication, however, I can't help noticing that, unlike my visit to the chain-link memorial, nothing here has brought tears to my eyes.

On the drive back to Washington, I dither. Is there a book here, and am I the one to write it?

I weigh the pros and cons. On the positive side, the theme is potentially moving– the aftermath of a mass tragedy that changed American history and its impact on a sweet country village. There will be many sympathetic characters, primarily those who are most affected by the crash. Finally, there is conflict, a necessary ingredient of all narratives, as bad actors attempt to stonewall the building of a memorial for their own ends. All told, it's a great American story, a verification that "the best America that ever was" is still alive out there in the heartland.

But there is a powerful reason for not taking on this project: I am very late in the game. There have already been two made-for-TV movies and one full-length feature film, and a few books, on the crash and its aftermath. My book will be different: It will be the first to chronicle the entire decade following the crash in depth. But at this late date, will anyone really care to read about how the federal government built a disaster memorial in the middle of nowhere?

And then there's the time and effort. This project, I tell Ann, could take me two years or more. (Actually, it will consume much of my life for the next four years and counting.) Do I really want to take this on?

"What else are you going to do with all that time?" asks Ann. Her question reflects a commonly held assumption: that a retired person can do anything he wants. Leisure (having no job you need to go to) is all you need. Right?

Well, not quite. As I will learn over the next four years, almost any creative endeavor involves some degree of that old bugaboo: risk. Take the seemingly benign project of writing a book, for example. Unless you are lucky enough to have an upfront commitment from a publisher (less and less common nowadays), authoring a book is one of the biggest investments of time and effort you can undertake, with absolutely no guarantee of a good outcome. It's a journey of faith, pure and simple.

Still, social scientist William Sadler said that it's important for an older adult to take those risks. That makes intuitive sense: I'm not going to discover my next creative flowering (if there is to be one) digging kitchen scraps into our garden plot. But if I knew just how bumpy the road ahead was is going to be for this retired editor aspiring to creativity, I might have stuck with burying those kitchen scraps.

CHAPTER 10

Flying Low
Over Shanksville

*Writing a book is a horrible, exhausting struggle,
like a long bout with some painful illness. One
would never undertake such a thing if one were not
driven on by some demon whom one can neither
resist nor understand.*
      —George Orwell

The prefab building perched on a hillside near the
memorial entrance is no place for concentrated reading, Every time the front door opens, a gust of cold air
blows across us. Nor do we ever get any real silence
because National Park Service staffers in nearby cubi-
cles respond to phone calls nonstop.

Still, I have to be here if I want to research the aftermath of the crash of Flight 93. The Park Service headquarters, the prefab building on the hill, is the only place
in the entire country where the archive of oral histories
is kept—hundreds of verbatim face-to-face interviews

with eye witnesses, first responders, family members, and anyone else who had a story to tell about the crash and their life journey going forward. The archive is a memorial in its own right.

The person who brings us stacks of oral histories is Kathie Shafer, who is also the staffer that has done most of the face-to-face interviews. A Shanksville native and wife of the local fire chief, Kathie is a soft-spoken woman whose blue eyes always seem to be on the point of tearing up. She is also a registered nurse who took a serious pay cut to work on the oral history project.

Kathie has traveled to the San Francisco Bay Area and Newark, New Jersey as well as all over her home county to conduct interviews face-to-face. She sits down with the interviewees to unpack the sometimes excruciating memories of September 11 and its aftermath. She always begins with the same question: "Can you tell me how your day began on September 11?"

For an empathetic listener like Kathie, the emotional impact of seeing the raw pain of grief, such as grown men breaking down in front of her, has been grueling. (I will learn that, as a general rule, the crash has borne down the hardest on the most sensitive individuals in Shanksville.) Still, Kathie told *The New York Times* that the oral histories are "probably the most important work of my life, other than being a mother and making sure my children are good citizens and good people."

As Kathie brings us a stack of oral histories, which Ann and I divide into two stacks, I can't help feeling that our visit is a very low priority at best. As editor of the landscape magazine, I had a corner office in downtown DC, and when I traveled for the magazine I was almost always a respected guest. Here at Flight 93, I feel like an uninvited nobody who's blown into town on the vague premise of writing a book.

Ann's willingness to read the pile of transcripts in front of us is an extraordinary act of wifely generosity. In fact, as someone unenthusiastic about long car drives, I wouldn't even have made the trek up here without her company. Ann approaches the task with her customary cheerfulness. She has just read a biography of Sophia Tolstoy, who edited and manually recopied all her husband's novels, and now Ann sees herself in a similar role. She smilingly refers to herself as my "editorial assistant." She scans the oral histories for nuggets that she thinks may interest me and sets them aside for me to read later as I plow ahead through my own stack, making notes and flagging pages for photocopying.

The aftermath of a mass murder doesn't make easy reading. Ann routinely sheds tears as she reads, sitting at the little table. Still, we persist.

The village of Shanksville itself, just a few miles down a bumpy road from the memorial, turns out to be a sad, left-behind place. The economy went belly up in the 1980s. All the coal was mined out, the small family farms couldn't make a go of it anymore, and virtually all the businesses left. The only store left on Main Street is a sandwich shop named Snida's. You can't buy groceries, fill a prescription, or gas up your car anywhere in Shanksville.

Whatever reverses the physical town may have suffered, however, the ethic of cooperation in the valley where Shanksville is sited appears to be alive and well. Helping your neighbor is still practiced in these Pennsylvania hills as it was when German settlers founded the village in 1789. The all-volunteer fire department, for example, undertakes hard, dangerous work for no pay. The community response to Flight 93 has tapped into the old values in a very serious way.

There's no denying, however, that Shanksville, at the beginning of the twenty-first century, is a sleepy hollow that has seen better days. Hardly anyone ever has a reason to visit the valley between the ridges anymore. "We were not even a spot on the map," says one resident. "We didn't know if we were connected, sort of, to the rest of the world." The Pennsylvania Turnpike isn't that far away, but few outsiders, pre-9/11, ventured down the bumpy, winding roads that lead to Shanksville.

The crash of Flight 93 changed all that. Suddenly, the eyes of the world were on this remote little village.

Shanksville's sudden awakening to global violence

turned its community upside down. Violent crime has always been so rare in Shanksville that there was no need for a policeman or a jail. Somerset County has always dutifully sent its sons off to war, but war had never come to Somerset County. Now, with unthinkable suddenness, the strip mine outside of town had become the scene of a mass murder, and the violence of the Middle East had stamped its awful footprint on the village's doorstep. "We've lost our innocence" became a common phrase around Shanksville in the wake of the crash.

"We're not—at least I'm not—versed in world events, and religious tensions in the Middle East," local resident Donna Glessner told a reporter after the crash. "For me to understand that there is this kind of evil in the world, this kind of hatred? I didn't know that kind of hatred existed."

As a visitor to these Pennsylvania hills, I can't help wondering if the "lost innocence" of the locals isn't a kind of naïveté rooted in a lack of curiosity about the larger world beyond these hills. Although no expert in geopolitics, I have been reading the morning papers long enough to understand that America has been far from blameless in our role in the Middle East. There was, for example, our destruction of democracy in Iran in the nineteen fifties and our support of antidemocratic regimes to this day. Not that this in any way justifies the horror of 9/11, but it provides a context. The good people of Shanksville, for all their red, white, and blue patriotism, seem to be unaware of that context. It seems that, the more time I spend in Shanksville, the less commonality of viewpoint I feel with these very kind, very decent, but politically naïve people.

Still, I have to admit that people like Kathie Shafer have a sense of mission about their project—something bigger than themselves that connects their little community with the larger, unblemished meaning of America. I, by contrast, am just a writer searching for his next muse. If I'm honest, my deepest desire is not so much to serve Shanksville or the memorial as to get back on the horse of writing.

A reader may wonder: given my ambivalence about the good people of Shanksville, am I the right person to write their story? I continue to believe that I am, because good storytellers have always been drawn to narratives rich in complexity and contradiction. This just means that writing a moving story out of such complex source material is going to be harder than I thought.

The most engrossing part of writing any nonfiction book is the research needed to support it, and I'm already deep into the research for this project. One book about the broader issues of memorial building into America leads to another, and I'm starting to get some surprises. From geographer Kenneth Foote's *Shadowed Ground* I learn, for example, that the contemporary obsession with building monuments to mass killings is a very recent phenomenon—really an anomaly in the history of memorialization.

Historically, the typical fate of the site of a mass killing was obliteration. No one wanted to preserve a memory so horrific. Take, for example, the apartment building in Milwaukee where Jeffry Dahmer dismembered his victims: It's been torn down. Likewise, the school in the Amish community in Pennsylvania where a gunman took hostages at a schoolhouse in 2006, and killed five little girls, no longer exists—the community razed the building. This is typical of a response that used to be almost universal. Those communities were, in effect, saying: Don't remind us of what is too grotesque or too painful to remember.

The opposite response to mass tragedy is what Kenneth Foote terms *sanctification*. This is the response to sites where a hero or heroes made a sacrifice that embodies some moral victory that transcends their deaths, perhaps marking a turning point in the history of the community. (The Gettysburg Battlefield is one great example.) Sanctification calls for a professionally designed landscape that typically includes a processional walkway, sculptures and statuary, reflective pools and fountains, and an interpretive visitor's center. Mass murders are almost never candidates for sanctification.

Oklahoma City, the site of the first modern terrorist attack on American soil, turned those categories on their heads. If there was there any transcendent moral victory in the Oklahoma City bombing that ennobled or redeemed those deaths, I am not aware of it. Nevertheless, Oklahomans demanded a massive, professionally designed memorial to commemorate the murders of their neighbors and loved ones. And that has become the model going forward, particularly for the sites of the 9/11 disasters. Nowadays, any mass killing, it seems, may be a candidate for sanctification.

The Flight 93 crash site, of course, stood apart from the other two 9/11 sites. Instead of going surprised and helpless to their deaths, the Flight 93 passengers stood up and fought. So, perhaps alone among the 9/11 sites, Shanksville was truly worthy of sanctification.

Still, I keep getting surprises—bombshells, almost— from the oral histories and other readings about Flight 93. We know, for example, what the passengers and crew aboard Flight 93 did: they revolted against their hijackers. That fact is known from the cockpit voice recorder. What we don't know is why they revolted.

Most Americans take as gospel the narrative, repeated by President Bush the day of the dedication— that the passengers and crew "rushed the terrorists to save others on the ground." Since then, the notion that the passengers and crew had willingly sacrificed themselves to save the people in the US Capitol and other civilians has swelled to the status of an American myth. When I mention that I'm working on a book about Shanksville, people I talk to infallibly express great admiration for the passengers "who gave their lives to save others."

But as I study the evidence from on-board phone calls or the cockpit voice recorder, I find no firm evidence to support the claim of self-sacrifice. Ultimately, I have to conclude that we just don't know why the passengers revolted. Family members I interview are also skeptical of the narrative of self-sacrifice. "I think they just wanted to get home," Gordie Felt tells me. And in his oral history Dale Nacke, the brother of Louis Nacke, who helped lead the passenger revolt, interpreted the passengers' motives as follows:

They were just people, people who came together and did the extraordinary. People who gave their lives to save, not necessarily others, because I think their motivations were very self-serving and why wouldn't they be? Do you really think that they were concerned about the Capitol? I highly doubt it. I'm sure they were trying to save their own lives, and that is the most powerful motivator imaginable. That, to me, is much more powerful than the touting of them as, "Well, they knew the plane was going to hit the Capitol." They didn't have a freaking idea where that plane was going. They came together as one to save themselves, and that is very powerful and very moving. And I am very proud of my brother for being part of it, as I am proud of everybody on that plane.

CHAPTER 11

Shanksville:
The Darkness And The Light

Outlining, researching, talking to people about
what you're doing, none of that is writing.
Writing is writing.
　　　—E.L. Doctorow

Finally, sitting down to write. But how do you start a book about one of the most violent events in American history that befell one of the country's most bucolic and most vulnerable places?

I'm clear about one thing: this will not be a turgid history tome. I will endeavor to write a nonfiction narrative that will engage and hold the reader much as a novel would. To do this, I'll have to follow what's been called the golden rule of creative writing: show, don't tell. This approach to writing is the stock in trade of good fiction writers and, starting with Truman Capote's *In Cold Blood,* it has become the model for nonfiction narrative as well. It involves "putting the reader in the scene" by clearly describing the sights, sounds, and colors of a scene, together with clearly drawn characters and believable dialog. All this while remaining true to the facts.

But how will I transform a vast trove of hundreds of oral histories into a readable, cohesive story? It isn't just a matter of cutting and pasting chunks of text together. Somehow I'll have to select, from thousands of pages of oral histories, the characters, scenes, and events that really tell the story from the inside. And, like old-fashioned prospectors panning for gold, for every nugget we hope to find Ann and I have to sift through hundreds of pages of transcribed interviews. Once I have those nuggets of the overall narrative, it's imperative that I craft them into scenes and dialog that draw the reader into the narrative. Here, for example, is the first scene of my first chapter:

It was a beautiful morning to be working on the roof. Not a cloud in the sky. When Robyn Blanset drove up to the farmhouse, her father, Ray Stevens, was already up there with his tools out, finishing work around the chimney. Robyn got the stroller out of her car and put her little girl, Twila, in it. Normally, she would give Twila snacks to keep her occupied while she was on the roof, but this morning a black cat wandered out of nowhere. The black cat was a stray who knew Twila, and it jumped in the stroller with her, giving Robyn an opening to climb the scaffold and set to work.

Like many of the scenes in the book, I base this one on Robyn's first-person oral history interview—Robyn and her father being two of first people to see Flight 93 come in low over Somerset County. And yes, the facts are exactly as Robyn reported them—I didn't make anything up. I simply paraphrase and condense her somewhat rambling oral history account into a brief scene that, I hope, captures the essence of her experience.

But why Robyn and not some other early witness? It was the black cat that got me—this dark omen of what we know is about to happen, juxtaposed against the vulnerable little girl in the stroller, all contrasted with the glorious sunny day. The incongruity intensifies as Flight 93 appears improbably low over the hill without Blanset and her father thinking there's anything amiss:

They heard its engines roaring before they saw it. Then, coming over the hill, there it was—massive, gleaming, and gorgeous against the bright blue sky. It was so low they could see the windows and the cockpit, and it occurred to Robyn that, if the passengers were looking out, they could see her and her father working on the roof....

"Twila, look up at the pretty plane," called Robyn, and Twila stopped fussing. But the big airliner had already disappeared over the next hill.

The chapter goes on to feature other scenes of eye-witness testimony from other locals who see Flight 93 coming over. But these, unlike Blanset and her father, realize that something terrible is about to happen. The climactic scene takes place in the office of the Rollock scrap yard where Nena Lensbouer had just brought a crock pot of food—more incongruity—so that her husband and the other workers could have a hot lunch. Chris Cordell, the owner's brother, who was watching the unfolding news on a portable TV, said the Pentagon had just been hit.

He no sooner said that—exactly at 10:03 A.M.—than they heard a huge screaming noise, like a missile in some television show. Then the office went dark, as if a giant shadow had passed over, and they heard something like what an atomic bomb would sound like going off next door. The building shook. When they threw open the door, all they could see was a column of fire down the hill that billowed more than three hundred feet in the air.

Two of the scrap cutters, Michael Shepley and Lee Purbaugh, were the only witnesses who saw the thing scream over their heads—so sudden that they barely had time to duck—and nosedive with unimaginable force into the earth. (As part of her oral history mission, Kathie Shafer would pursue them for months, seeking an interview. Neither of them would sit for it.) The scene proceeds with Nena Lensbouer, holding her cell phone, running alongside her husband downhill across the trenchy ground, scattered with rocks and debris from the abandoned strip mine.

> *If a plane crashed, thought Nena, a former fire-fighter, there has to be someone down there that needs help. It seemed to take forever to get down to the crash site, even though it was only two hundred yards away. The 9-1-1 control center wouldn't let them hang up.*
>
> *What do you see? They kept asking. Tell us what you see!*
>
> *"Well, the trees are on fire. We see smoke from the ground. There's some debris hanging, like papers and stuff."*
>
> *What about the plane?*
>
> *"We don't see no plane."*
>
> *There has to be a plane!*
>
> *But there wasn't one—just a big hole in the*

ground that was on fire. They walked right up to
the hole and looked down into it. Nothing. They
hollered and screamed, but no one answered.
They ran into the nearby woods, which were
burning too, looking for survivors. There they
found lots of scrap metal and debris, and lots
and lots of paper, but no people—not even a body.

Granted, this is strong stuff to open the first chapter of a book, and it will probably put off sensitive readers from reading further. But I'm writing this to fulfill my intent of telling all the darks and lights of the story, including the most horrific parts. If those opening scenes are a little too macabre and might stop some readers in their tracks, there are many uplifting and inspiring scenes in ensuing chapters. For example, here is the first visit of the bereaved family members to Somerset County, just days after the crash. I base this scene on two oral history interviews, one from family member Allison Vadhan, the other from Shanksville native Judi Baeckel.

The bus ride began in tense silence. Everyone
on board knew that they were going to see the
mass grave of their loved ones. Allison Vadhan
of Atlantic Beach, New York, whose mother had
died in the crash, was on one of the buses. She
hadn't wanted to come. What was the point of
going to Pennsylvania just to stare down into a
hole? But friends convinced her that if she didn't
go, she'd regret it someday. So here she was, on
the bus with other families of the victims, rolling
through the Somerset County countryside. Then
they started seeing signs and American flags on
the country roads, hill after hill, and signs that
read "Thank You," "God Bless America," and

"Never Forget."

*The caravan rolled into Shanksville. The tiny
village was adorned with red, white, and blue
wreaths and flags hanging out of windows or
on fences. A church group was there with a big,
folded American flag, and dozens of residents
gathered between houses. One of them was Judi
Baeckel, who stood in her front yard just to show
support.*

*When the buses began to weave their way
through the village's narrow streets, lots of people
waved, but Baeckel thought that waving might
not be appropriate. So she stood with her hand
over her heart—because her heart was breaking for the families. The windows on the buses
were dark, and she could hardly see anyone, but
when she saw someone wave, she waved back. Or
somebody would blow a kiss, and she'd blow a
kiss back. But mostly she just stood there with her
hand over her heart.*

*Then the locals unfurled the big flag, and a
Shanksville woman started singing "Amazing
Grace." In that moment, a bond seemed to form
between the bereaved families and the people of
Shanksville. We are with you in your sorrow, the
locals' eyes and waving hands seemed to say. We
will stand by you for as long as it takes, for whatever you need to make it through this.*

Like a compelling novel, a nonfiction narrative needs
a few finely drawn, believable main characters. In the
aftermath of the crash, a wealth of characters will
emerge who will briefly populate my account, but there

_____

are a couple who stand out as emblematic of important aspects of the response to the crash. The most import- ant of them, to me, is the Hick Coroner.

In a county where neighborly generosity is the norm, not the exception, the Hick Coroner—Wally Miller's own self-deprecating term for himself—is the person I'll come to regard as the most sterling example of bedrock generosity in responding to the bereaved families and overseeing what would come to be known as the sacred ground. (As a reminder, he was the speaker who wept so bitterly at the memorial dedication.) I introduce him in a scene immediately after the crash.

Miller was a first responder who, as he drove to the crash site, seriously doubted that he was ready for what he was about to see. He had only dealt with two murders in his entire career, and a mass murder like this was unthinkable. How many bodies would he find?

But once at the site, he walked for an hour before he saw his first recognizable body part, a piece of spinal cord. He sensed not people but their absence—a sign that the passengers "got snatched out of their bodies really quickly." It dawned on him that he wasn't going to play the usual role of a coroner dealing with bodies but rather a cemetery full of vaporized remains.

Later that day Miller, who had always been ter- rified of public speaking, was called to make his first media statement. A big table was filled with microphones, and the journalists were five deep. But Miller stammered his way through the interview. Next there was a feature article about

*him in The New York Times. From then on—
after the FBI had combed the site for evidence
and departed—he became the custodian of the
site and the public face of caring for the sacred
ground.*

*He also became the spokesman for the crash
site, fielding interviews that took up three or four
hours every day. Miller found the media hoopla
annoying and was no respecter of celebrities.
When superstar TV anchor Katie Couric showed
up with a camera crew and wanted to film
directly on the crash site, Miller refused.*

*"I'm not letting you walk on the site," he said.
"You can walk over there, but this is sacred, hallowed ground."*

*Miller's real role, as he saw it, was to be there for
the families. Another coroner advised against
getting too close to the volatile family members
of mass murder victims. But Miller made it his
personal mission to contact the family of each
victim. Not all wanted to talk to him, much less
make the long journey from California or New
York to meet him on that desolate hillside. Others, however, made the trip, hoping Miller could
help them understand what had happened to
their loved ones. Ultimately, there were hundreds
of face-to-face meetings on that hillside.*

*Why did Miller create this mountain of extra
work for himself? "I wanted the world to realize who we are," he said. "We might be hicks, but
we're hicks who know what compassion is."*

So it may come as no surprise that I want to make Wally Miller a key figure in my book. I met Miller at the dedication and asked if I might interview him on my next visit to Shanksville. He readily agreed. So each time I visit the crash site I call his coroner's office and try to set up an interview.

It's going to prove more difficult than I imagine.

If people like Wally Miller and Kathie Shafer channel the tragedy of Flight 93 into constructive action, the tragedy takes a few people in Somerset County into a mind state that looks more like obsession. One of these is Terry Butler, among the eye witnesses to the airliner as it passed high above him toward its doom.

I've come to see Butler at his workplace, Stoystown Auto Wreckers on the Lincoln Highway. He greets me amid a sea of wrecked cars. I feel an immediate sympathy with him, a powerfully built man with bright blue eyes and a graying ponytail. I ask what his specialty is at the yard, and he proudly tells me that it's removing windshields from wrecked vehicles. He readily agrees to talk to me at the end of his shift.

The setting for the interview turns out to be the strangest place for an interview I've ever been in. We get in Butler's old van and bounce down the rutted dirt tracks of the wrecking yard, past acre after acre of carcasses of battered automobiles. Looking straight ahead over the steering wheel apparently makes it easier for him to talk about how the crash of Flight 93 has changed him.

Helplessly viewing the final descent of Flight 93, it seems, has tapped into some deeper sense of psychic insecurity that just won't let go. Our conversation takes place more than a decade after the crash, but his voice still cracks when he talks about it. "I'm always told we are supposed to move ahead and try to forget," Butler tells me, "but I don't know how. I saw it right there." He still tenses up when airliners bound for Pittsburgh fly over. "I don't think I'll ever get over this."

Butler's personal memorial is his own body. Tattoos cover both arms from wrist to shoulder, and he has cut off the sleeves of his shirts for all the world to see the tattoos. Butler got his first one less than a year after the crash. "It was only supposed to be one tattoo," he says, "and then it just evolved into all this—artwork." Butler's imagery reflects the standard vocabulary of Flight 93 tattoos: a fireman and a crying Statue of Liberty, along with a pair of eyes over a verbal description of what Butler saw in the plane's final dive. Butler even welcomed the discomfort of the tattoo process because it brought him closer to the Flight 93 victims. "You've got to take pain," he says. "Forty people took pain."

Still, Butler's obsession, if that's what it is, has given his life meaning and purpose. He has consecrated his life to ensuring that everyone he meets remembers Flight 93. "I just don't want people to forget" is his mission and mantra.

The more I learn about Wally Miller, the more the bedrock decency of his character shines forth. Take this scene, which I paraphrase from his oral history interview.

> *One day Wally Miller received a call from the White House. As a first responder, he was invited to a concert at the Kennedy Center for the Performing Arts in Washington, DC, that September, and as a special honor the White House invited him to sit in the box with the president.*

"Wow!" said Miller. "I've got to tell my wife—we're going meet the president."

"No—not your wife. Just you," said the White House staffer. "This is just for first responders. She can sit down below, but we want you to sit up in the president's box."

"My wife handled every remain that came out of there," said Miller. {Miller's wife, Arlene, worked with him at the family funeral home. She had been so inspired by his example that she had gone to mortuary school to learn the profession.) "I'm not coming if she can't come."

"Rudy Giuliani's girlfriend's not going to be in the box either," countered the staffer.

"Well, it's important what you just said," Miller replied. "It's his girlfriend. This is my wife. I'm not coming without her." And that was the end of it. Miller didn't know who went to the concert in Washington, but he didn't go.

The dance to arrange an interview with Wally Miller is becoming more and more awkward. Each time I'm in Shanksville and call him, he is with a bereaved family member. Being rebuffed for an interview is a new experience for me. When I was at the magazine, people were generally receptive, even eager, when I called. It's particularly dumbfounding in Miller's case because he gave hundreds of interviews in the first two years after the crash. Never turned a request for an interview down. So why now, and why me?

After a few rebuffed calls, it's becoming obvious that he's beginning to see me as a nuisance. On my last call, he almost hangs up on me, and I realize it's over. I've simply come on the scene several years too late. Whatever the reason for this rebuff, this first big disappointment of my Shanksville journey will sting for a long time.

By now I am two years into research and writing, and I only have a couple of draft chapters to show for it. I thought I'd be done by now—a year to do the research, a year to write the book, I told myself. And here I am with only two draft chapters. When I wrote for the magazine, I was a marvel of productivity, but on this book I seem to be dragging along at a snail's pace. Only rarely do my sentences and paragraphs seem to sing on the page. Hardly ever do I feel warmed by the ever-distant fires of creation.

Someone once told me that, of all the arts, the one that offers the most immediate gratification is dance. Based on my own experience, music must be close behind. But of all the arts, writing is undoubtedly the most likely to feel like work. The gratification typically comes more in the finished product than in the creative process. In the case of my Shanksville book, I am starting to wonder if the subject matter is the problem. The topic that at first seemed so bright with interest now seems to have lost its luster.

And I am haunted by the feeling: *Time is not on my side.* Thirteen years have passed since the crash. I know that the farther this book project goes from 9/11, the more my book will be old news to anyone in the reading public. Two other books about Flight 93 and the crash site come out as I toil away at my writing. One is an academic treatise focusing strictly on the chain-link memorial, the other a (to my mind) glib overview of the doomed flight and its aftermath by a marketing professional from Pittsburg. As if in personal insult, it appears in my local branch library.

This book is a journey of faith, and my faith is wavering. I don't have a publisher lined up who is champing at the bit. There is no foundation funding me and expecting a finished product at a given date. The Park Service, while perfectly cooperative about letting me visit their headquarters and read the oral histories, is completely hands-off as to whether my project lives or dies. In short, I'm just an out-of- town journalist trying to write a book that no one has asked for.

But at least I am far along enough to put out a book proposal.

CHAPTER 12

The Fiddles Of The Palisades

There's deep strength in failure. It's a gift to fall down and get up. Failure makes us familiar with the actual possibilities that come from risk and robs our fears of the power that comes from the unknown.
—David DuChemin

Back in DC and back to music, I finally get my big chance to play before a live audience. After years of playing at Hell's Bottom, Ed Shaeffer, who scoured me so fiercely in my early efforts there, has asked me to "sit in" with his band when they perform at Los Nopalitos, a Mexican restaurant in Silver Spring. "Sitting in" involves coming up to the bandstand to play a tune or two or three with the paid members of the band. It's a mighty step forward from only a few years ago—I'm publicly showcasing the harmonica in a bluegrass setting. This is big!

In the dusky light of the restaurant, I survey the band members--Barb on bass, with a hot-pickin' banjo player and an equally hot mandolin player whom I've met before and a gray-haired fiddler from Philadelphia whom I haven't—as they wind up the first set. Decked out in a white Stetson hat, Ed is in his element, cracking jokes off the cuff and tackling the vocal chores with his fine voice. After a break, he calls me up for three instrumentals.

How strange and thrilling to be in front of a microphone again looking out over a crowd. My downtime has lasted way too long. But when the band launches into "Cherokee Shuffle," and my turn to solo comes around, I lean into the mike and blowdrawblowdrawblow across the brass tines of the harmonica, and the tiny instrument sweetly sings out this wonderful old fiddle tune. When I conclude my solo, I get a smattering of applause that lies sweetly on my ears, and Ed casts a surprised look—a compliment of sorts—my way.

Next we play the classic fiddle tune "Liberty" (I forget some of the notes, but it's not a disaster), and finally "Midnight on the Water," a beautiful old waltz that climbs up high and sweet and leans on almost every available note on the harmonica, and once again my solo gets applause. As I exit the bandstand, Ed loudly calls out my name to the audience as if I were the night's celebrity. This is a moment that any harmonica player must savor in full awareness, because invitations to sit in with a band are few and far between. So yes, Bill, savor this moment, this sweet milestone in your crooked journey into bluegrass—but how can you learn to find joy in the music without that terrible craving to be in the spotlight?

Part of the answer may lie in musical confabs where no one gets to be in the spotlight—ever. Today I'm looking for that situation in the Palisades, a comfortable residential neighborhood in the westernmost corner of the city, on the high bluffs overlooking the Potomac River, where a jam consisting entirely of old-time American fiddle tunes is open to all.

It's four years now since I walked out of my job at the landscape magazine, and I have devoted part of my free time to learning how to play fast-paced fiddle tunes on the harmonica. I now have a small repertoire of tunes under my belt from the bluegrass jams, but what I am walking into today will be fiddle tunes wall to wall. And most of them I will never have heard before, much less sat down and practiced. This is an unexplored country, and there's that sinking feeling again in the pit of my stomach.

The music room of the house is a sunny space, glassed in on three sides. Three concentric circles of folding chairs point toward the spot where a leader will sit. Musicians file in and take up their chairs, at least eight of them with fiddles, but others with five-string banjos, guitars, and mandolins, and a couple of hammered dulcimers.

Clearly, I have wandered into a musical anachronism. The old-time barn dances of frontier America in which the fiddle was the main instrument are part of American history. Yet the music stubbornly hangs on, sustained by fanatical devotion of players and listeners, mostly in comfortable suburbs or urban neighborhoods like this one, far from the hardscrabble lives that gave birth to this music.

As I take a seat, I already feel dreadfully out of place. Most of the musicians seem to know one another and are chatting amiably. I sit silent and awkward, and not simply because I don't know a soul here, but because what I'm going to attempt to do is so far out of the norm. How did I get it into my head to aspire to be one of the few people in the entire country to be able to play fast-paced, acrobatic fiddle tunes on the ten-hole harmonica?

The jam leader enters the room. He's Ken, a well-known fiddle and hammered dulcimer player from Baltimore. A slight, spare man in his middle years with a ready smile that helps calm my nerves, he doesn't waste much time—after tuning his fiddle, he launches into the first tune, without bothering to name the tune, or even what key it's in. Everyone recognizes it, though, including me: It's "Angeline the Baker," that same tune that I played at the VFW and that I know by heart.

What's immediately obvious is that old-time music is a completely different animal from bluegrass. Whereas in bluegrass the tune is passed around a circle, giving each player a chance to interpret it in his or her own way, in old time style the all the musicians play in unison—the same tune, the same way, over and over again. It would be boring except that the melodies themselves are beautiful, and the act of playing exactly in time and in tune with others is really difficult. The goal is not to stand out but to lock in with the rhythm and the note-for-note melody line of the fiddles. Still, as the jam surges forward—a huge sound, a roomful of instruments playing the same country dance tunes over and over—I hang in there and discover that the effect can be hypnotic, almost trancelike.

Although most of the tunes are new to me, I can hear and isolate a repeated phrase each time it comes around. And if I can hear it, I can often play it. So even if I can't fully reproduce a tune that I have never heard, I can find a wedge into it. It is like panning for gold. At a break between tunes, one of the string players jokes, "The chair of the harmonica section did pretty well on that one."

The next tune is completely inscrutable. "Oklahoma Rooster"? Never even heard of it. A problem I quickly discover is that old-time fiddlers seem to take delight in calling the most esoteric, little-known tunes—and there are hundreds for them to choose from. So I pick up my mandolin and begin to search for those ever-elusive off-beat chords: chunk-chunk-chunk. As I relax into the felt rhythm, the woody offbeats of the mandolin carry my brain to a place where the ancestors live—the very earli-est percussionists drumming on hollow logs at the dawn of humanity. The sound of the fiddles is a surge of melody that obliterates the beat of the song, so I have to listen with full attention to the clawhammer banjos and the guitars, straining to hear the all-important first beat of each measure, the key to where I'm to chop on the off-beats. It's an exercise in intense listening where there is no thought, no critique, and the *I me mine* is completely subsumed by the *We*. Nobody stars. Nobody has to star. As the afternoon plays on, I feel a quiet elation just to be part of the old-time cohort.

But I still have some unfinished business with the bluegrass community. Call me pigheaded, but I can't let go of the dream of finding a place for the harmonica just because it's not one of the standard instruments.

The next Sunday afternoon at Lyon Park, I get my chance to make a last stand. A bearded young fiddler is leading "Soldier's Joy," a tune I have practiced many times with backing tracks. I stand expectantly in the circle, waiting my turn to solo. But, as has happened too many times before, the fiddler passes right over me.

I feel that familiar flush of hot indignation. *Dammit, I know this tune! I can play it as correctly as anybody here.* But the solos have already gone past me around the circle.

There comes a time in the life of every harmonica player when the 97-pound weakling of the musical world has to step up and make a stand for himself—or just slink away and accept that he will never, ever have the chance to play on the varsity team. There's one last, risky card I can play.

When the tune comes back to the fiddler and he plays "Soldier's Joy" through one last time, I jump in without asking permission. I play loud and forthright right over his solo—a terrible violation of bluegrass etiquette—but doubling him note-for-note.

The man's eyes get very wide as he stares at me over his fiddle. When the last notes of the tune ring out, fiddle and harmonica in unison, I fully expect him to angrily scold me for barging in on his sacred solo. Instead, he breaks into a surprised grin, while some of the other pickers laugh out loud, and I understand that I've passed some kind of test.

I have no illusions that I have slain the dragon of rejection forever. There will be many snubs on my journey ahead. But this afternoon at Lyon Park, I ran the fatal risk and have come away unscathed.

CHAPTER 13

As The Eye Awakens

*The object, which is back of every true work of art,
is the attainment of a state of being, a state of high
functioning, a more than ordinary moment of
existence... We make our discoveries while in the
state because then we are clear sighted.*
—Robert Henri

It's a lovely afternoon, and Ann and I are walking in
the Fern Valley at the National Arboretum, locked in a
lighthearted debate about the relative difficulty of knitting—Ann's passion—and my drawing the human form
from direct observation. I patiently explain that drawing, as an art form, is dependent on the indefinable
quality of individual talent, while knitting is a rote skill,
something anybody can learn how to do it in an afternoon or so.

"Not just anybody," she counters. "I'll bet you couldn't
learn how."

I chuckle, because I know from my experience of

drawing people how hard it is to get a recognizable likeness, much less to go beyond the likeness and extract
some inner essence of the personality of the sitter. Even
people who have years of art training can't always do it.

"Well, what do you think would be more valuable, on
a cold night in the woods," Ann asks, "my knitted scarves
or your art?" So much for artistic snobbery when talking
to a knitter.

But seriously, what is the value of drawing, cold
night or not? The art of drawing, particularly drawing
from life, is so anachronistic that one wonders why anyone devotes time and attention to it in the twenty-first
century. Software exists nowadays that can translate a
quick snapshot into an accurate line drawing without all
the long effort of learning to draw. Anyway, I don't want
to make the mistake of thinking that because something
is difficult and takes a long time to learn, it is therefore
of great value.

One obvious difference between knitting and drawing is that one is solitary, the other social. There may be
twenty artists in the life drawing studio, but each of them
is in his or her own little bubble, too deep in concentration to carry on anything resembling a conversation.
Knitting, by contrast, is typically very chatty and very
social. Lives can touch other lives.

My drawings, so far, are touching almost no one but
me.

The lounge of the homeless newspaper vendors
is a very laidback and untidy place. *Street Sense* is the
newspaper that the homeless themselves write, and this
room in a downtown church is where they can find a
quiet hour away from the bustle of downtown sidewalks
where they hawk the paper—their sole, precarious livelihood. Most days, the only activity in this lounge consists

of vendors trolling the internet on a couple of in-house computers, munching snack foods, or dozing.

This afternoon, however, is the one when Ann teaches homeless women how to knit, and I've tagged along in hopes of sketching them. The women cluster around a long table where big colorful skeins of acrylic yarn are spread out, Ann has brought coffee and sweet snacks too—essentials to tempt the vendors to attend class.

These women are the human rejects of a city that worships wealth and success. Many of them are plagued by mental illness, substance abuse, prison records, abusive spouses, and racism. Many have no family who cares whether they live or die.

If you look closely, though, you may see other dimensions of their lives—for example, the innate eloquence and strength of their faces or the grace of their hands and fingers as they wield the knitting needles. That's why I'm here—to sketch them, with their permission of course. As I take a seat off to the side, my drawing pad in hand, I'm reminded once again of the first gift of sketching people in public: that the act of intense looking reveals the beauty even in the most ordinary face. And these women's faces are far from ordinary.

The way Ann teaches is hands on, literally. She sits next to each of the women in turn, puts her hands over their hands, and moves their fingers in the knitting sequence while repeating the instructive limerick: "In through the front door, circle around the back, peek through the window, out jumps Jack."

Teaching knitting to homeless women is a far cry from Ann's former occupation--running an agency that organized fundraising campaigns to arts organizations and environmental groups. She managed a staff of twen-

ty-five from her office overlooking the National Geographic headquarters. By the time she sold the business and retired before her sixtieth birthday, however, Ann had been deeply influenced by our Buddhist sangha and Hugh's teaching of compassion for all living beings. That brought her to the downtown church, where she handed out papers for the vendors to peddle on the street. That led to these classes to teach the vendors how to knit. Both activities are "a way of opening my heart," she says.

Today, while my eye is concentrated on sketching the women, my own heart opens just a crack. A vision flashes across my mind's eye: that of an iceberg in the Arctic Ocean. The life histories that separate these women from me—homelessness, substance abuse, mental illness—are the nub of the iceberg visible above the water. The iceberg's vast underwater bulk—loves and hates, vulnerabilities, fears and hopes—are all feelings that we share: our common humanity.

With that vision, I feel an upwelling of empathy with these women. I don't do anything with the empathy, though. I just keep on sketching. Maybe that's my loss.

Ann is acting on empathy.

As the philosopher Bertrand Russell grew older, he described how he achieved personal happiness: "Gradually I learned how to be indifferent to myself and my deficiencies; I came to center my attention increasingly upon external objects: the state of the world, various branches of knowledge, individuals for whom I felt affection."

If Russell was right about happiness in old age, then I, in my gimlet-eyed pursuit of self-expression, am seriously on the wrong track. But right or wrong, maybe that's the track I have to travel. Maybe anyone who's born with the creative itch is somehow meant to take that unique and reclusive journey. For better or for worse.

Except that I do have these moments when I connect with another soul through the medium of drawing. As I get in the habit of carrying a sketch pad with me everywhere, other drawers occasionally notice. One day on a crosstown bus, an African American man sitting opposite wearing a workman's uniform speaks up. "I noticed your drawing pad," he says. "I draw cartoons." He opens his own sketch pad, full of facsimiles of Disney characters. "But I'm having trouble drawing noses. Can you show me how to draw a nose?"

I feel a flash of recognition; here's a kindred spirit with the same yearning to draw that I have. I've worked hard at my own drawing journey, but at least I have the leisure and the resources to take art classes. He doesn't.

"Look," I say, sketching a rough triangle with my pencil. "A nose, if you look at it head on, is just a triangle. Some noses are broad, some are skinny, but they're still just triangles. The same if you see it in profile--it's another kind of triangle." I demonstrate, again with a rough diagram.

He gets it. As I exit the bus, I look back and catch him sketching a face in profile—and the nose is a believable nose. It's a sweet moment, sharing my love of portraiture with another aspirant. But again, I don't go looking for shared moments like these, teachable moments where I touch other lives. I am still too laser-focused on expressing the craving self.

Back at my life drawing sessions, I am nagged by what Marcia said in the sangha: that the act of making of art should be its own reward. That seemed a pious platitude at the time, but later I wonder: what's stopping me from finding immediate satisfaction—it's currently called the "flow" state—in the act of drawing itself?

The flow state was first identified and described by psychologist Mihaly Csikszentmihalyi as a state of intense, energized absorption in a challenging activity that requires total concentration for its performance. The flow state is generally experienced as highly positive, often enjoyable, and sometimes ecstatic. I know what the flow state is because I have begun to experience it in my musical events. When it's my turn to solo and I'm playing at the very limits of my ability (or a little beyond my limits) in a supportive group of musicians, I experience a state that transforms an ordinary jam into something radiant—what I call that "walking on air" feeling.

Csikszentmihalyi wasn't the first to identify such states, of course. There was, for example, the artist and art teacher Robert Henri, who described "a state of high functioning" in his 1923 book, *The Art Spirit*. Surely there were many others who described similar states.

Up to now, though, I haven't experienced anything like that in my life drawing studios. I've been too focused on getting an accurate likeness with all proportions correct and the lights and shadows where they should be. In short, I'm focused on the product, the outcome. There's a tightness, a rigidity, about my effort that tends to cancel out the possibility of flow.

One Friday, at the life drawing session at the Washington Studio School at Dupont Circle, I meet someone who offers me a hint of a way forward. Martin Campos, an artist from Philadelphia, has come down to lead a workshop over the weekend. In his late forties, Campos' dark hair and beard are already flecked with white, attributed, no doubt, to how hard it's been to pay the rent while remaining true to his art vocation. This afternoon he's chosen to sit in on the life drawing session.

I choose a seat next to Campos as the model takes her first pose and I peek over at what he's drawing. If he minds my looking on, he gives no sign—he's fully absorbed in his first sketch. I first notice the minimalism of Campos's materials: a box of six chalk pastels and a sheet of toned paper. Picking up a pastel seemingly at random, he draws it across the paper in small, rapid strokes, and a vague facsimile begins to emerge in patterns of lights and darks. Campos makes no attempt to get a likeness, and the figure that flows from his pastels lacks an arm or a leg, or even a head. The lack of figuration surprises me, because Campos was trained in the tradition of traditional representational painting at the Philadelphia Academy of Fine Arts, where he now teaches. What unfolds from the chalks in Campos's fingers is a semiabstract meditation on the body in front of us. It contains a form memory of the model, but transformed into something rich and strange.

At the end of the session, Campos hangs around to talk expansively to us sketchers about his artistic journey. He grew up in a conservative Hispanic community in New Mexico where his talent for drawing emerged early. He honed his drawing skills in life drawing sessions like this one, where he gained a high degree of mastery in the accurate representation of the figure.

When he enrolled at the Philadelphia Academy, he thought his figure drawing skills would find their ultimate expression. There, however, a teacher encouraged him to let go of his technical mastery and to "make a mess and find your way out of it."

"What if you don't find your way out of the mess," I counter. "Isn't it important to end up with a drawing that really sings?"

"You have to give up drawing something pretty," Campos says, "and focus to recording just what you see and sense in that communion of sight, trying to have a dialog with the model. Be willing to wipe out a drawing if you sense you are going astray from that felt seeing. The real gem of it is that you're reacting to a moment. The moment is the most important thing in your drawing. It's all about risk—about seeing and connecting with what you see. Not about garnering praise or prizes. For me, it's almost a religious vocation."

Not about garnering praise? Campos' words kick open a door in my mind. If the key to making art is running the risk of failing in order to enter into what he calls a communion of sight, is that communion something I could possibly touch into?

I'm going to find out on an upcoming Friday afternoon back at the Studio School, when Kenyatta, a very slim African American woman I have gotten to know a bit, is today's model. It helps me that she's a neighbor, living with her parents and her teenage son just a few blocks from me and Ann.

Enter into a communion with the model and don't think of anything else, I remind myself as Kenyatta takes her first pose. I draw a deep breath, and my mind goes back to that darkened room at the Buddhist meditation where I centered down, sat on the straight-backed chair, and followed the rhythm of my breaths. I remember how the eternal procession of thoughts slowed down and found their place of quiet. If I can find that quiet place in myself again, right now, I can focus just on Kenyatta's grace and the vulnerability and let that become my only study, the only thing that matters in the world for the duration of the pose.

Kimon Nicolaïdes, in that first, pivotal lesson that got me drawing seriously, wrote that I should just touch the edge of the figure with the tip of my pencil and slowly move the pencil along the curve of the figure. (If this sounds lurid, it is not. Drawing well takes far too much concentration for prurient thoughts to dominate.) I keep my eye on the model, not on the paper, only glancing down to check if my hand isn't trailing off somewhere. If a thought intrudes--How well am I doing? Will I garner acclaim and accolades?-- I'll take another breath and let those thoughts find their place in quietness. For the thirty minutes of this pose, I can be right here, right now, where nothing matters in the world except the posed figure in front of me and the tip of the pencil gliding across the tooth of the paper, searching, searching, searching for form.

Then the pose is over Kenyatta puts on her robe, and I walk out into the stairwell to stretch.

What just happened? Something, some tension in my head just let go. It wasn't an epiphany exactly, but it was a small opening, maybe a way forward. Can I find that opening again? We'll see.

I go back to the studio and look at my drawing. Actually, it's quite a good likeness.

But that wasn't the point, was it?

Still, my art journey can't just be a marvelous communion of sight known only to myself. Art was meant to be shared. This is where I'm stuck. I have to make the dreaded step from creating my art to sharing my art. It's scary because, first, I have no experience in promoting or marketing anything, and second, I shrink from the possibility of rejection—once again, the abhorred risk. Yes, I could enter a framed drawing in annual shows, but what if my entry is rejected and I have to go down and ignominiously cart it home?

One sunny evening in May, I am sketching a band led by a bass clarinet and a tenor sax player at a Take Five concert at the National Portrait Gallery when a big fellow carrying a camera passes by and asks if I am going to be sketching through the entire concert. At a break he sits down next to me, introduces himself as Bruce, and leans over conspiratorially.

"What are you going to do with your drawings?" he asks.

"Not sure."

"Could it be you're just stacking them up in your basement?"

I nod. (And yes, the piles of drawings are mounting up.)

"Do you ever give them to the band?"

"No. How do I know they'd even value them? I'm not a famous artist."

"I'm sure they'd love to have them. Even if you are not the greatest artist in the world, you are way better than anyone they are going to get to draw them." Bruce (a museum volunteer and self-described hack at photography) tells me he keeps a website with a massive collection of photos of events and people, some of them famous, he has photographed. He shows me a sample on his cell phone.

"Never be afraid to show your art," he says as he drags me around to meet the band. But it's all too sudden, too fraught with the possibility of rejection, or what is almost as scary, accepting my drawing with sniffs of condescension. This sensitive plant couldn't bear that. So I thank Bruce for his advice and flee into the May evening.

Over the next weeks, however, Bruce's advice makes more and more emotional sense. *I just hate to see artists selling themselves short,* he said, which is exactly what I have been doing.

One bright Saturday, though, the fates conspire to give me a shove in the right direction. At a festival of finger-picked guitar music in Takoma Park (a tribute to the late, local guitar legend John Fahey), I sit on the front row beside the town's outdoor gazebo listening to Don Bikoff , who played guitar in the Greenwich Village folk scene of the 1960s and is still actively playing well into his later years. The joy of making music shines out in every note that Bikoff plays, and it occurs to me that here is a shining example of an artist, well along in years, who is experiencing fruition in the very act of playing.

As I listen to him pick, I sketch his head, and hands holding his guitar in colored pencil, and a simple line drawing of the long-limbed, white-bearded Bikoff quickly emerges under my fingers. An exact likeness it is not, but my spontaneous line work captures some of the energy and passion of his finger-picked guitar playing.

"Your drawing is beautiful," comes a voice of a woman sitting behind me. "Don's my cousin. I'm sure he'd love to see it." So, with that gentle push, I approach Bikoff where he's mingling with the crowd after his set. I hold up my drawing, very sheepishly.

"Your cousin said you might like to see this," I say.

"You should have given me more hair," is his smart-aleck response, but then, "What are you going to do with it? I'd like very much to have it."

"Trade you for a CD," I say. That just popped out of my mouth. And Bikoff walks over to his stack of CDs and gives me not one but two. It's a sweet moment, exchanging with an artist in another genre. So begins a regular practice of sharing my drawings with musicians in future sketching forays at folk festivals and jazz concerts. Reactions vary, of course. Most are delighted to see a good likeness of themselves drawn with a certain feeling. A few don't understand what they're looking at, but no one is ever angry or upset. Many snap pictures. And a few offer to trade a CD for a sketch.

I'm learning that the goal is to get my drawings out there somehow or other, not to garner blue ribbons for them. Above all, I'm not hiding them away in a dark closet anymore.

CHAPTER 14

Expectation And Its Discontents

No one has ever lived in the past or the future, only the now.
—Thich Nhat Hanh

If there's a moment of truth for any author, it's the moment he or she steps away from the safe haven of the writing desk and into the uncertain waters of seeking a publisher. After toiling away at the Shanksville book for nearly three years, this moment has now come for me. I've got a solid outline and a few good chapters in hand, and I must now chance it all before the unforgiving eye of the publishing industry.

On another writer's recommendation, I hire an agency to send a synopsis of my book proposal to publishers and agents through their network of contacts. The agency does its job, and the initial response to my synopsis is good—many of those contacted ask to see the sample chapters. From several of those who read the chapters I responses like this one :

You're a fantastic writer and the first chapter is just amazing, superb, heartbreaking.

With a tribute like that, you'd think my inbox would be overflowing with offers to publish. Not so! The agent goes on to write:

But you haven't convinced me this could work for a trade press. I think the editors will all feel this is an absolutely brilliant long form article for the New Yorker, but that there isn't enough at stake for a book to reach a large audience. Most of the "memorial" books you cite are with university presses, and that is telling. To me, there would be an audience for a broad history all about memorials, what we mean by them, how we design them--but to focus on this one story is too specific to attract a large number of readers.

And that's the most encouraging of the responses. I create a file folder on my laptop for rejection letters. It quickly balloons.

One offer to publish does come through. It's from an academic press in North Carolina, but their main interest is in the word count. Their sole stipulation is that the finished book contain at least 75,000 words so that they can market it as an academic text and charge a goodly sum for it. But I never intended this to be an academic book! I am writing it to (hopefully) reach a wide readership and to touch readers' hearts, not just to end up as a footnote in some dissertation. So, even if theirs is my only offer so far, I can't go with them.

So it seems I've wasted that money on the agency, and my spirits are at their lowest ebb since I started this project. Yet I trudge on and finalize my research, which means that Ann and I have to make yet another trip to Shanksville. This project, it seems, is no longer about the love of the journey. It's about getting to the finish line. I set out to write something beautiful, but a lot of it feels like drudgery without a support system and without a near end in sight. After a long day of reading oral histories, Ann and I stand in the parking lot of the Park Service headquarters. We're both tired, and Ann breaks the silence.

"Bill, if you having this much trouble finding a publisher," asks Ann, "do you really want to keep grinding away at this project?"

The question catches me off guard. Strangely enough, I have never considered the possibility that I should just chuck the whole thing. What about the investment of time and effort, all the long drives to Pennsylvania, all the long hours sitting at the little table in that drafty room. After all that, don't I deserve, damn it, some return on investment?

What might that return look like? Anything beyond publication is a little vague at this point, although I do assume that I will be invited to speak at landscape architecture departments at universities (I know a few heads of departments from my work at the magazine) and at local bookstores. That, and maybe speaking at historical societies in Pennsylvania towns. And at the Flight 93 visitor's center—that's a given.

But if I'm honest, there is a more deeply personal reason for finishing the book: I don't want to stop being a writer. I don't want to give up my role as the artist who, toiling away in the seclusion of his study, pieces together language and scenes that may move and inspire legions of readers. As someone who has always loved the work of great writers, I want to keep at least a toehold in that glorious fraternity.

"I want to keep at it," I finally say. "I want to finish the book and I want to do it right. There's a great book in here somewhere."

There in the parking lot, I cast my lot with the desperate hope that, if I just persist long and doggedly enough, something beautiful will come of this. At this point, hope is all I've got left.

Sometimes the most obvious solutions elude us. Now that my nationwide search for a publisher has turned up nothing, I have the overdue idea of querying Penn State University Press. Why didn't I think of the Pennsylvania connection before?

What makes it all the more likely is that, at Penn State for another purpose, I once met the publisher. I email him, reminding him of our meeting. He puts me in touch with the press's acquisitions editor, Kathryn. After reading the draft manuscript of the chapters I've completed so far, she calls me—a very empathetic, warm voice— to say it looks like a good fit for the press's Keystone series, a line of nonacademic, accessible books intended to serve the citizens of Pennsylvania. "I'm very excited about the book's potential," she tells me.

Before I declare victory, though, there's another hoop to jump through. Kathryn will send the mostly completed manuscript to a knowledgeable reviewer for comment—a standard and perfectly reasonable step. I wait, brimming with optimism for the first time.

CHAPTER 15

The Shanksville Redemption

Not all boats which sail away into darkness never find the sun again.
—Stephen King

Alas, any optimism is premature. When Kathryn's anonymous review comes back, it's trenchant.

"The manuscript lacks sufficient details," writes the reviewer. "The author uses vague modifiers." Both charges seem unfair and even incorrect—but then I'm an author responding to criticism.

Other comments are downright catty: "The book could have local appeal; become the kind of book someone might buy at a county fair along with some pie." Ouch!

I suspect that the reader is a landscape architecture academic who knew me in my role at the magazine and holds a grudge against me for some reason—although that may be the paranoia of a disgruntled author. But surprisingly, the reviewer ends by recommending publication, with substantial revision, of course. First and foremost, I must write an in-depth profile of the village of Shanksville, which no one has written to date.

After my initial outrage, I reluctantly admit that this mandate makes sense. But this will require yet another trek to Shanksville—and I am now into my third year of this project, which I expected to have wrapped up a year ago.

By this time I have become a little obsessed by the mounting travel expenses of this project—costs I may never recover in royalties. It isn't that I can't afford the trips—I can, easily. It's that, with each trek to Shanksville, shelling out for another motel stay and another tank of gas hammers home the fact that this project is a journey of faith, and it's all on my own nickel.

So, to save a few bucks, what about sleeping in a pup tent in the local state park? To my surprise, Ann consents to this nutty proposal. (Is there no limit to what this woman will endure for her quirky husband on our shared journey of investigation?) So we pitch our tent, and everything is going well until—as if to punish my miserliness—the air mattress deflates in the middle of the night.

Still, the trip turns out to be very worthwhile, because unearthing the history of Shanksville will add a fascinating layer to my research. The problem is that almost nothing about the town's history exists in print. My good fortune is that Donna Glessner lends me her copy of *Reflections of Stonycreek 1776-1976,* a locally written and published booklet now so scarce that Donna insists that I read it without leaving town.

Reflections of Stonycreek is a revelation. From it I learn that Shanksville hasn't always been the bedraggled place that it is today. The booklet paints a picture of a village centered on a thriving region of family dairy farms, founded as part of a wave of German immigration that began while America was still a British colony. In 1798 one Christian Shank built a grist and lumber mill on the banks of the Stonycreek River and laid out a few streets and home sites. People began to move in, and eventually there were two blacksmith shops, a brickyard, a two-story general store, and even a small hotel and bar. A local dairy shipped butter all the way to Baltimore in fifty-pound kegs. A doctor set up his practice in 1840. The townspeople even provided their own entertainment: a 1919 photograph shows the 22-piece concert band, every musician in uniform.

The village never grew beyond a few hundred people settled between two ridges, but it thrived right up until the late 1970s. By then it enjoyed two grocery stores, a service station, an automobile dealership and garage, a barbershop, and a modern bank. Coal mining surged after World War II, incorporating huge draglines to strip the soil and mine out the seams.

But then the coal played out, and with it the best-paid jobs. The family farms went the way of family farms all over the United States. As the local economy tanked, virtually all the local businesses moved out, even the service station. Finally, even the barber closed up shop. Residents had to commute to work far from the village, if they were lucky enough to find work at all in Somerset County, which even today has one of the least vibrant economies of any county in Pennsylvania.

Today, it's hard to imagine that a hotel or an auto dealership could ever have existed in Shanksville. I can imagine the bank, because the building still stands there, empty, and across the street from it the barber shop, also empty. It's sad but not surprising: Shanksville has met the fate of towns all over the United States that were founded on family farming and resource extraction and today are almost ghost towns.

For me, though, this overview of history is the last link in my research, and I feel a certain satisfaction, a sense of completion, as I hand the booklet back to Donna and Ann and I head home down the old Lincoln Highway.

What I don't know is that this is the last time we will make this drive, the last time I will ever visit the memorial or Shanksville. I always assumed that I'd come back for a book signing or a talk at the local historical society, but no such thing is in the cards. I don't know it as the memorial recedes in our rear-view mirror, but I will never see Shanksville again. This is goodbye.

Back at my writing desk, I'm making a concerted push to finish the book. As I muster my thoughts and research and plow forward toward a conclusion, however, I am haunted by a persistent question: what can I finally say about the logical culmination of the whole process—the built memorial? More broadly, are massive concrete-and-stone memorials like this one, complete with fully decked out visitor centers, really the best means of preserving a national memory—or are they just very expensive anachronisms? Two made-for-TV movies and one full-length Hollywood film, *United 93,* have been made about the passenger revolt. In an age of electronic storytelling, might these be more stirring reminders of those moments of terror, courage, and resolve than an inert memorial?

Then there's the design of the memorial itself. In the modernist tradition of abstract minimalism, it is devoid of patriotic inscriptions and heroic imagery that might remind a visitor what may have happened on board the plane and how the passenger revolt averted a national catastrophe. I happen to like the Flight 93 Memorial's austerity because I can supply my own narrative about what it means. I don't need anyone telling me what to feel or think.

Many Americans, I suspect, crave that imagery and those inscriptions. One example is the public reception to the World War II Memorial, dedicated in 2004, on the National Mall. The design has been roundly panned by architecture critics for its garish, bombastic display of gilded eagles, bas reliefs of tanks and warships, and inscriptions of great allied victories—and yet it is one of the most visited and loved memorials by the American public. On a sunny afternoon, the throngs of visitors resemble an outdoor celebration.

By comparison, what are visitors' reactions to the Flight 93 Memorial Plaza? Those who've come to the Plaza since the dedication tend to be predisposed to reverence for what had happened here. The actual design of the Memorial Plaza, however, is receiving mixed reviews from visitors. Some have written on TripAdvisor, the online public comment site, that the memorial is "unfinished," even "temporary," as if that stark line of black concrete alongside the sacred ground is somehow not the "real" memorial. Representative comments include "hallowed but lacking," "anticlimactic," and "very stark."

Comparisons with the old chain-link "people's memorial" simply won't go away. One longtime ambassador, Chuck Wagner, can't help but notice the difference in visitors' reactions. Of the temporary memorial, he tells me, "A lot of tears were shed there. You don't see much of that anymore—not the heartfelt connection that there used to be."

It all comes down to a final, more sweeping question: was this memorial really worth ten years' work and sixty million dollars? For me, the jury is still out. If I am honest as a writer, this book is not going to end as a resounding affirmation of much of anything, except the profound decency of the people of Shanksville.

And what can I finally say about the sweet village itself? Will any of the thousands of visitors to the memorial make a detour to the isolated village?

Not likely. Tourist traffic to the memorial has been diverted away from Shanksville, which means that visitors can come and go on the well-paved Lincoln Highway without passing through the village. It is only two miles away from the memorial, as the crow flies, but by car it's a fifteen-minute detour down a bumpy two-lane road— and anyway, there's nothing worth seeing when they get there. Travelers, should they choose to stop by, still can't gas up their car in the village or spend a night there. Any economic windfall from tourist dollars will never flow to Shanksville, never lift it out of its economic stagnation.

So how might I end this book that begins with the murder of forty people and ends with a memorial of uncertain value? Surely not with a patriotic flourish—a speech from the dedication, for example. Better to end the book as quietly and respectfully as I possibly can— not on the day of the dedication, but months later, in the dead of the Shanksville winter.

One frigid day in December following the dedication, a blue pickup truck with a brightly painted "Let's Roll" insignia drove down the snow-covered hillside toward the Memorial Plaza. When it came to rest in the parking lot, Terry Butler stepped out and walked out along the plaza, an envelope in his hand. He bent to leave it in one of the receptacles hollowed out of the wall for tributes. It was a Christmas card addressed to the heroes of Flight 93, a remembrance of what they had done for his country, the sacrifice to whose memory he had consecrated his life. He had left a card like it at the temporary memorial every Christmas since 9/11, and now he left one here, at the black Memorial Plaza that stretched out under the December sky. But it was too cold to linger in this place, and Butler walked back to his truck and drove away across the vast, snowy landscape.

CHAPTER 16

To Publish And Perish

People and events don't disappoint us, our models of reality do.
—Stephan Zweig

As soon as I ship the expanded manuscript to Penn State Press, I get a thrilling phone call from Kathryn. They want to publish!

It will be a small paperback, she says rather apologetically, with black-and-white photos and maps. No matter—I'm ecstatic.

Well, not completely ecstatic—the marketing department doesn't like my proposed title, The Wound That Binds Us. Yes, it's enigmatic, but I think it captures the emotional crux of the story—bereaved families and an empathetic community finding common ground in the face of a great tragedy. Too vague, says marketing. They propose *From Memory to Memorial*, which, to my ear, sounds pedestrian and predictable, even though it has the virtue of saying exactly what the book is about.

But I'm not going to fight the marketing staff—they know something about selling books, don't they?

Kathryn mandates a hard deadline: all the images and any final rewrites must be completed by Christmas. There's a compelling reason for this: all the copy editing, indexing, and formatting must be completed in early spring so that the book can be printed by August to be ready for the fifteenth anniversary of the memorial and the inauguration of the visitor's center—the final, essential component of the memorial. It's an opportunity not to be missed, and I set to work, writing or rewriting chunks of the manuscript and gathering in maps and photographs.

Finally, I pen the dedication, the only dedication that could ever make any sense: *For Ann, who was with me every step of the way.*

The Christmas deadline mirrors my mood exactly: I'm like a kid waiting for Santa to come down the chimney. What could possibly stop me now?

What could stop me is the copy edit. Penn State is an academic publisher with rigorous standards of footnoting and other forms of attribution. I am familiar with such standards from my graduate school days, but my work on the magazine has accustomed me to a much looser process.

One morning in January, Kathryn gives me a disquieting phone call.

"We noticed some . . . carelessness in a few of your attributions ," she says, "and, as we dug a little deeper, we uncovered other problems. Frankly, if these were an academic book, we'd ask you to go back to the drawing board. But this book is in our Keystone series, so we'll proceed and try to fix the problems as we go forward."

"Going forward" involves an excruciating copy edit. A laser-eyed (not to say obsessively nitpicky) copy editor insists that I document every interview, news article, book, online reference, and oral history. That may seem like reasonable scholarly practice, but I've lost the sources for some of these and have to track them down, and the copy editor then has to take a further step of verifying that the citation was what I said it was. Do the editors suspect me of plagiarism?

The entire process drags on for five weeks.

Finally, one last chore: the index. I call Kathryn to protest that I don't want my book to be seen as an academic text but as an emotional piece of narrative nonfiction. So why does it need an index?

"Every title Penn State publishes has an index," is Kathryn's final word. She gives me the option of hiring a professional indexer (pricey!) or doing it myself.

Compiling an index is exactly the nitpicky kind of work for which I have absolutely no taste, but again Ann comes to the rescue. She's an organization and detail person, and we sit together in front of the laptop computer for three full days alternating between the search function in our word processor and double checking citations on handwritten lists.

Indexing the book ourselves was supposed to be about saving money, but when all this is said and done, what I'll remember most is the experience of sitting side by side with Ann in front of the laptop, assembling all those index citations.

"We make a good team," says Ann, to which I silently echo, *Ann, you don't know how right you are.*

But the copy editing process has kicked publication into another time zone. I email Kathryn: Are we still going to publish by September 11? Her response—*I'm afraid not*—hits me like a gut punch. I'll be missing the best marketing opportunity—the fifteenth anniversary of 9/11 and the inauguration of the visitor's center. The book will come out in spring of next year—eight or nine months behind schedule. A marketing person writes me a conciliatory letter, but by now my high-flying spirits are dipping dangerously toward the ground.

Finally, the following spring, the long awaited book comes out—and yes, it really is, (in my eyes at least) a perfect, beautiful baby. The writing that I toiled over for years now sings on the page. Even the cover—a photo of a Shanksville man wrapped in the flag and holding a sign that reads I DID NOT FORGET—captures the commitment with which Shanksville met the disaster.

But the satisfaction of seeing the finished work is followed almost immediately by disappointment as the baby goes out into the world.

I send the cover image with a note to the heads of landscape architecture departments at universities. I've been on friendly terms with these people for years; surely there'll be at least a couple of invitations. Not a single person even deigns to respond. I send complimentary copies to the Shanksville natives like Donna and Kathie in gratitude for their help, but from them I hear not a peep. Fortunately, the leaders of the memorialization effort, Gordie Felt and John Reynolds, to whom I send copies, respond with glowing tributes.

Requests to talk about the book at Pennsylvania historical societies and local bookstores run into brick wall after brick wall. Not even my neighborhood library, which hosts weekly book talks, shows an interest. In short, I've put a beautiful, perfectly formed baby out into the world, and almost every door she tries to open is closed to her.

A marketing person at Penn State wangles an invitation to Good Day PA, a daytime ABC-TV show in the Pennsylvania capital, Harrisburg. Ann and I drive up, unsure what to expect.

Good Day PA is a surreal experience. I'm given a three-minute slot between a Girl Scout troop hawking cookies and a cook demonstrating how to make your own pasta. The emcee, a petite woman more at home with the Girl Scouts than an author, hasn't done her homework, but I'm primed to talk about the book, and the TV crew, to their credit, has loaded still images of the memorial to compliment the interview. For a three-minute slot, it goes reasonably well.

A year later my first royalty check from Penn State will confirm that fewer than five hundred copies have been sold, rather than the many thousands I pridefully expected. Worst of all, my sales rankings (the bellwether of success or failure) on Amazon are in the toilet.

It never was about the money. I would be completely happy if I found out that thousands of readers had checked the book out of libraries or borrowed them from friends and gleaned something from reading them. (The last part is key.) But to think that my beautiful child is wandering out in the shades of anonymity is nearly intolerable.

With brutal terseness, Ann captures my disappointment: *all that work.*

What keeps me from jumping off the proverbial bridge are the reviews. No, I don't get a review in *The New York Times,* but the evaluations in scholarly journals and homegrown Pennsylvania publications are all positive to stellar. The most prestigious review, I suppose, appears in a history journal from the University of California, but the most gratifying is by a reviewer in the Johnstown, Pennsylvania magazine who writes that reading it made her cry. For a book that I thought I drenched in emotional scenes, that is, frankly, what I hoped to hear from a reader.

The reasons for the book's relative invisibility, are, no doubt, related to failures of marketing and other factors that, as an author, I don't understand. But I do know, have known for a while now, that time was never on my side. For the wave of interest in all things 9/11, I am more than a decade too late.

Looking back over the last four years, I should have heeded signs that I knew were there. The crooked road to find a publisher. All those polite letters of rejection. The almost general lack of interest in the project from any institution, including, most tellingly, the Park Service itself. Those were the signs, and they were pretty clear.

If I could go back in time to that moment in the parking lot when Ann asked me that hard question—"Are you sure you want to continue slogging away at this?"—what would I answer, knowing what I know now? With the gift of foreknowledge, I might just have said, "You know, I think I'll just call it quits. Better to spend those thousands of hours on something that yields more creative satisfaction."

But, here I am, stuck with a beloved orphan into which I poured four years of work. Where do I go from here?

CHAPTER 17

The Road Ahead

*Uno cree saber lo que busca, pero solo al final,
cuando lo encuentra, sabe lo que realmente andaba
buscando. Y bien podria ser que lo que rige el
destino del hombre no sea Cristo ni Jupiter ni Ala
ni Moloch sino Pachacamac, el dios de los avances
hacia ninguna parte, el dios de la sabiduria que
llega un dia despues del fracaso.*
["You think you know what you're looking for, but
only at the end, when you find it, do you know
what you were really seeking. And it may well be
that what guides the destiny of man isn't Christ or
Jupiter or Allah or Moloch but Pachacamac, the
god of going nowhere, the god of the wisdom that
comes the day after failure."]
—William Ospina, *El Pais de la Canela*

Every story—the stories in books, the stories of our
lives—can be seen as a narrative arc. The arc typically
begins with a status quo, which represents stasis and

stability, such as my fulfilling career at the landscape magazine. Then something occurs to shatter the status quo and trigger a quest toward some new, unknown destination. The tension builds slowly, through fits and starts, toward a climax at which the protagonist, after a long struggle, finally achieves a signal victory. It's the highest point, and often the most ecstatic point, in the action. Whether the protagonist wins or loses, the laws of story dictate that he must absorb some critical lesson and change in some fundamental way, fitting him for the next life stage or the next journey

That model exactly fits my journey into the art of narrative nonfiction, with one important twist. Yes, there was a signal victory and a joyous climax—the publication of my book—but it was followed by an abrupt reversal, a sense of expectation thwarted. It feels less like a climax than an anticlimax.

It's becoming more and more clear that writing the book, and the other creative activities of the last few years, were a response to my resignation, on a matter of principle, from the job I loved. I have never regretted my decision to resign in the way I did, but the abruptness of the transition left a vacuum in my soul. To move forward, my intuition was that the healthiest, most life-affirming way I could imagine to fill that vacuum was by diving as deeply as I could into the creative arts. That intuition was right on target. What I didn't realize was that a vocation for the arts—a beautiful, wondrous thing, no question about it—could carry with it some onerous side effects. In my case, one of these has been an intense yearning for recognition for my creations. When these haven't come my way, I've suffered the pain of disappointment and even resentment.

I've been desperately looking for a new place in the

sun. Nothing I've tried has taken me there. So what have I learned and how have I changed? Will I end up just another disgruntled old-guy writer sucking on a sullen beer in his living room? God, I hope not.

Sometimes you can learn a thing or two from others who have walked a mile in the same shoes you're wearing. One such person is Hayden, a bearded retiree whom I know from my Quaker meeting. Hayden has found a satisfying late-life career as an urban tour guide, where he can make use of his encyclopedic knowledge of the physical fabric of Washington.

Hayden loves to track down arcane bits of Washington history, to delve into yellowing documents in the basements of city and federal archives for forgotten bits of local lore. To that end, he spent four years researching and writing a book about, of all things, the history of Washington dog pounds from 1785 until the early 1940s. Today we're traveling by Metro train to visit a historic Hebrew cemetery in the Congress Heights neighborhood on the far eastern edge of the city. The hero of Hayden's book, Samuel Einstein, the city pound master from 1872 until 1912, is buried in the cemetery we're about to visit. On the way, we talk about our books and their receptions.

Not surprisingly, Hayden got no takers to publish his dog pound book. Eventually, he self-published it with the giant online bookseller, which has emerged as a viable option for authors who can't find an opening in the labyrinth of traditional book publishing. Online publishing carries no guarantee of literary success, of course. I ask Hayden how many books he has sold in the year or so since he published it. He laughs.

"Do you have two hands, maybe three? That many fingers is how many books I've sold."

I don't have the heart to ask Hayden how much he's earned in royalties. We both know that writing the book was never about the money. Hayden is happy that least his book is out there. I ask him if he has any regrets for the four years of work for so little fame or reward.

"None at all," he says. "I really just enjoyed the research—getting down into the archives and poring through them. That, to me, was a reward in itself. The thrill of the hunt—it was a kick!"

I wouldn't have found some of Hayden's findings exactly "a kick," but Hayden has a taste for arcane statistics. How many dogs were there in DC in 1900? What do tax rolls tell him about the sale of dog tags in a given year? If that sort of thing brings Hayden joy, more power to him.

I, too, found my research—well, much of it was sad, but all of it was fascinating. Grief psychology. The history of disaster memorials. Historic trends in the decline of rural America. I'd delve into one book or news article, and it would lead me to another intriguing line of investigation. That's one reason the book took so long to complete. A key difference between my research and Hayden's, though, is that he approached his with a lightness. I, on the other hand, always had an eye to writing a magnum opus, finding a publisher, maybe winning an award. Not exactly a light-hearted "kick" at all.

Nevertheless, the Shanksville book—if I could just look past my dashed expectations—was a success on many levels. I did achieve my stated goal—I wrote something beautiful, if only in my own eyes. It was published by a reputable press, and it garnered five-star reviews. I think I honored the Shanksville residents and the families without sugarcoating their story.

Would I do it again? Probably not, but I always knew

it was a risk. And the nature of any risk is that you never know how an enterprise will turn out—otherwise it wouldn't be a risk. So was I right to take the creative risk? Absolutely!

In the end, my beautiful baby (beautiful to me, anyway) is alive and out there in the world. And knowing that, I'm ready to march forward into Life After Shanksville.

Still, I must face the hard truth that my life as a writer may be over. Oh, I may jot down some memories, as I'm doing in these pages, try to make a reckoning of my late-life journey. But sallying forth to tackle complex, demanding issues? All that is probably over for me.

What then? So much of my identity has been that of a writer, the solitary artist piecing together words and paragraphs to convey story and feeling, to somehow convey the depth and complexity of the human story, the wonder of being alive. If that's over, what remains? If not a writer, who and what am I?

Well, for one thing, I am a father. I have two beautiful grown children, both of whom are doing well in their lives. I will admit that, when they were kids, I was too often absent, probably when they needed me most. I was trying to piece together a new career and a life for myself after my first career had gone sour. Helen bore the brunt of raising the kids, and for a quirky child of the sixties playing the role of mom in a conservative Southern city, I would say she did a wonderful job.

While I was writing my Shanksville book, Helen died after a long-drawn-out bout with cancer. Emily and Chris showed what they are made of in in her last months, going above and beyond the usual filial roles to spend time caring for her and track down a last-chance cancer specialist in Ohio. My only role, at the end, was to pay for an airline ticket so that the specialist could treat her and, when that treatment failed, to pay for her cremation. It wasn't much, but at least I could do something.

Helen's funeral was held on a fishing pier on Folly Beach outside Charleston. I chose not to attend, but Emily and Chris were there, to let her ashes sift down into the Atlantic Ocean as she requested. I am so very proud of both of them.

Chris and I have continued with our separate musical journeys because music, which should have brought us together, hasn't succeeded in that role up to now. But this November, Ann and I are celebrating Thanksgiving at Chris's home in Florida, and I have a chance to test whether that chasm can be bridged. We're here for our annual family reunion, an event we've been trying to piece together every year, with varying degrees of success. This Thanksgiving we've gathered at Chris's stucco-clad home. Chris is now married to Kristina, a native of Orlando, and the marriage seems to be working. Chris is happy and loves living between the Indian River and the Atlantic Ocean, where he can indulge his passion for water sports. I don't share that passion, but I absolutely love the vast expanses of sea and sky.

Chris is still devoted to playing his solitary guitar. He plays every day, sometimes for hours on end. Some of the time spent is practicing scales and modes, the building blocks of music. His playing continues to improve. The surprising thing, to me, is that he's completely content to practice tirelessly in his living room, finding "success" in seeing his playing improve and seemingly indifferent to the goal of turning heads or garnering accolades. He finds satisfaction in music for music's sake, a seemingly pure and abstract pursuit.

This afternoon, Ann and I have just come back from a walk on the beach. When we come in the house, Chris is sitting in his sunny living room, surrounded by his three dogs. Kristina is in the kitchen, getting a head start on fixing Thanksgiving dinner. Emily and my grandkids are, as usual, out by the pool. Chris's guitar is close at hand.

"Chris, want to play a few songs?" I ask, trying to not let my eagerness, my vulnerability, show in my voice. After all, there's no guarantee that this father and this son may finally find some common ground, after all those years when the chasm between us lay so wide and deep. Maybe today, though, we can take a last stab at bridging that doleful gap.

"Sure, Dad," he says, and I take a deep breath. I know that Chris is most at home in the intricate chord changes of contemporary rock songs. So I break out my battered mandolin as Chris launches into Gregg Allman's "Melissa."

I've never been a fan of rock music and have never played this song, which tells the mournful story of a gypsy who rides the rails from coast to coast, always longing for his lady love, sweet Melissa. I don't know the chords or even the key as Chris launches into it, but I've been jamming so long with the bluegrass guys that I am sometimes able to follow intuitively where the melody and the chord changes are going. As Chris picks with a comfort born of long familiarity, I begin to weave in melodic riffs and fills aimed at harmonizing with Chris's chord changes—and it doesn't sound half bad. So after all these years of musical separation, have I learned to be versatile enough at music to harmonize with my own son?

As I dig into the mandolin strings, improbably the answer seems to be yes—to my ear, anyway, I'm finding the licks that fit well into the spaces between his vocal lines.

Family is a big part of what life is all about, but the way we live now, family seems such a tenuous affair, people living so far apart, the bonds always at risk of shredding and fragmenting. Sitting in Chris's living room, I have no way of knowing how long our annual reunions will continue, how many more times we'll pick out tunes together. This afternoon, though, that's all in the future, the future that we can't know. All we have is this palpable Now, and all that really matters is this moment, this shining—and dare I say loving?—moment.

> *In deepest dreams the gypsy flies*
> *With sweet Melissa*

As Chris begins to sing out that final verse, our past with its sadness is nowhere to be felt. This song that we share is all there is. I lean toward Chris and dig into the mandolin strings one final time as the last chords chime out into the Florida afternoon.

I am also a husband, and as I go further into my seventies, that is increasingly the part of my life that matters most. After a lifetime of unflappable health, I have experienced some recent symptoms that are currently only nuisances but that feel like intimations of mortality. My time on this earth is not going to just roll on forever, and this realization has had the remarkable effect of opening my eyes and ears and heart wider as I go through each day.

One quiet summer day, I spend the morning working on these pages. Then Ann and I drive to our intensely planted community garden plot and pick fresh basil and tomatoes for dinner. After our garden duties, we decide to take a walk through the wooded valley that borders the garden. By mutual agreement we start the walk through the woods by different routes. Ann chooses a paved sidewalk, whereas I love to cross the stream that lies at the bottom of the valley. But we always meet at a fallen tree. "See you on the other side," calls Ann as we part.

As I walk down to the stream and tiptoe across the stepping stones, Ann's parting words haunt me like a grievous refrain. *See you on the other side.* Suddenly, it's as if I can glimpse the future, that sad future when we'll be parted by the paths of time, when there won't be another side to meet on. By the time I meet Ann at the fallen tree, my eyes are awash with tears.

Ann refuses to be dragged into my sad vision. "I'd rather focus on this moment we're living right now," she says. "Look at this beautiful day. We're having a wonderful walk through these woods. Isn't it better to focus on that?"

With that, we link arms and continue our walk through the forest, together. I try to recall a quotation from the Buddha to cap off this moment, but the wording escapes me. Better to just walk.

Still, as my seventh decade increasingly tugs at me, it's becoming more and more clear that at some point, I will be separated from everything I love. I am a transient being, caught in the web of time and fate, a pilgrim in this land, just passing through. Given that blunt fact, one thing I can reliably do is to relish each moment as it flies by—to focus on cultivating the habit of being in the here and now.

But what does that mean in practice? "Being in the moment" is a slippery goal, but I do know what it's not. It's not spending your days responding to texts on your cell phone or endlessly making to-do lists. not wasting time and energy on mulling over some past resentment or counting on some future happiness that may or may not come to pass.

Instead, it's about stopping to smell the white perfection of a magnolia blossom in June, being grateful to be able to walk through the intense, life-giving green of the National Arboretum on a sunny afternoon, absorbing the touch of a loved one's hand in the middle of the night, keenly aware that such moments may never be repeated.

One of those moments comes thanks to my Quaker meeting's spiritual development program, which sponsors weekend retreats at a wilderness location overlooking the Potomac River in rural Maryland. During a break at a retreat I wander down into the woods.

As I descend, I come upon a natural spring flowing out of a bank where someone has set up massive blocks of stone in a very sculptural composition. I have no idea what the practical purpose of the stones may have been, if any, but to my eye it looks like an altar. And above it, sitting on a low branch and clearly visible to the naked eye, sits a scarlet tanager—a bird, I am told, that is rarely seen at close range. The sight cancels out all thought, and a sense falls over me of a sacred Presence, some impersonal Oneness that is both very much of this moment and yet completely transcends time. Whatever it is, I am transfixed—I could not be more spellbound if a voice spoke to me out of a burning bush.

Then the bird takes wing, and the spell is over, but for that sacred moment I have been there: I have seen the winged vision over the altar near the great river, and now it's time to return to the everyday, to retrace my steps back up the path to the retreat.

I began this five-year journey into the arts expecting a new growth spurt in the third stage of my life. How has that panned out? Have I progressed in drawing, music, and writing in these last five years?

Take drawing, for starters. My personal assessment is that my ability to draw portraits and people in action has improved by leaps and bounds. I can now capture a recognizable likeness and a model's facial features and accurately delineate the proportions of the human figure with expressive rendering of light and shadow.

I'm amazed that in my mid-seventies I actually seem to be *getting better at something*. As the doors of midlife vigor close ever more tightly behind me, other doors, creative doors, appear to be opening.

It's finally sinking in that art's transforming power occurs in how one holds the experience of making art, not in any hoped-for masterpiece. The act of drawing from life is an exercise in the sacred act of paying attention, whether my drawings garner oohs and aahs or not.

Writing is a harder nut to crack, because the doing of it so rarely yields immediate experience of "flow." (Writing these pages has been a welcome exception, probably because I'm just telling my own story.)

But it's from music that I have gleaned the most spontaneous joy. In contrast to arts in which approval can come (or not) long after the creative act, just being allowed to play with musicians more accomplished than oneself is a triumph in itself. And, after many rejections and other hard knocks, I have learned how to access the "flow" state in music, not just occasionally, but quite often. I regularly have that "walking on air" feeling on leaving a jam.

It's important to realize, of course, that in the larger scheme of things these jams don't amount to a hill of beans. There is no audience, no adoring throngs to listen and applaud, no audio technician to record this for posterity. And that realization is actually freeing. Somehow, in each never-to-be repeated musical gathering of kindred spirits, something satisfies that hunger I seem to carry around—the compulsion, if you can call it that, to bring out some feeling hidden deep inside of me, into the singing light of day. And yes, I am increasingly confident that I can lead a song and that others will lean in to harmonize on the chorus. I find it amazing that a seventy-year-old tin sandwich player can raise a joyful noise with a bunch of pickers and singers years younger than he is. So, despite setbacks and dashed expectations, the creative flow can still grow and flourish late in life. (By the way, in jams with musicians fifty years my junior, I have never felt singled out or rejected because of my age.)

But the sound I always come back to is the wail of the 10-hole harmonica, the sound I first heard live from Neal Pattman in the basement of that school cafeteria. That is the sound that brings me home. And yes, I am beginning to find greater acceptance for that sound, once seemingly taboo, in bluegrass sessions around town. One sunny September afternoon, I have a chance to make that joyful noise once again. There's a bluegrass jam outside the Atlas Brewery on the eastern edge of the city, out near the Anacostia River. For once, the jam has an audience—a crowd of beer drinkers lounging at picnic tables around us.

The impromptu band consists of all local "hot pickers", a couple of guitarists, a banjo player and a mandolin player, a bass, and finally, a slight, dark-haired woman who is new to me but is said to be a hot fiddle player.

Someone calls the "Red Haired Boy," a modal, haunting, Celtic-derived fiddle tune. The band kicks it off at breakneck pace, and the guitar, the mandolin, and the banjo each take a turn playing a fiery improvised lead.

Just keeping up with the racing tempo is a challenge.

Then the dark-haired young woman begins to preach on her fiddle, and suddenly we're not just on a street in Washington DC, we're on one of those mountain ridges not far to the west where the laurel grows in the shade of the oak and the hemlock, and where my mountain forebears managed to scratch out a hard-won living. If sparks could fly from an instrument, they'd fly from the strings of this woman's fiddle, backed by the pounding rhythm of the band. Then she concludes her breakneck lament, and it's my turn. I lift the tin sandwich to my lips.

As my septuagenarian lungs find the strength to puff out a mighty rhythm of inhales and exhales, the tiny brass tines of the harmonica buzz and begin to sing, and I'm on that mountain too, calling out that same sad and lovely lament that my forebears would have found so familiar. *Blowdrawdrawblowblowdraw* in a frantic but precise melody line that lies against the rapid-fire chord changes of the band in a sweet, sad, and intimate embrace.

The Buddha taught that life is only lived in this very moment—this transient, irreplaceable moment with its unique texture and color that will never come again. The trouble is that we so rarely give this moment our full attention, our minds too often lost in remembrances of things past and expectations of things to come— in my case, the expectation that someday I would win the acclaim, the blue ribbons that I thought I so richly deserved.

But on this shining afternoon, as the "Red Haired Boy" reaches its fiery crescendo, there is no thought, no expectation, and no memory, only the intense consciousness of this moment, and this moment is as bright as the sun over the Anacostia. Blue ribbons be damned—

the grand prize for years of paying my dues is just to be in this place with these kindred spirits, breathing this music into the September afternoon.

TO THE READER

Thank you for reading my memoir. If you gleaned anything worthwhile from it, I have a favor to ask: Please write a reader review on Amazon.com or Goodreads. com. It doesn't matter if it's long or short, just whatever you honestly feel.

And always feel free to find me at my website, jwilliamthompson.com or contact me at my personal email, landcommentator@gmail.com.

www.ingramcontent.com/pod-product-compliance
Lightning Source LLC
Chambersburg PA
CBHW061819040426
42447CB00012B/2733